②

publisher
MIKE RICHARDSON

editor
TIM ERVIN-GORE

designer
DARIN FABRICK

MEGATOKYO™ VOL. 2

Published by
Dark Horse Comics, Inc.
10956 SE Main St.
Milwaukie, OR 97222

First edition: January 2004
ISBN: 1-59307-118-3

3 5 7 9 10 8 6 4 2

Printed in Canada

megatokyo

②

story & art

FRED GALLAGHER

co-creator

RODNEY CASTON

"shirt guy dom" comics by

DOMINIC NGUYEN

www.megatokyo.com

dark horse books™

This book is dedicated to:

The Megatokyo community for your unwavering support and faithful readership. Without you there would be no Megatokyo, and I'd still be scribbling in the dark.

All my friends, family and fellow conspirators who have helped make Megatokyo what it is. I can't thank you enough for your hard work and support.

Sarah -- my conscience, my muse, my angel. That's way too much work for any one person :)

CONTENTS

MT_vol_2_fr33talk.txt

Hi, welcome to *Megatokyo* volume 2.

If you are a *Megatokyo* reader and have been following the comic online, then you should be familiar with much of what is in this book. It contains Chapter 1 and Chapter 2 (that's comics 134 to 306 -- June 2001 to September 2002),as well as most of the other content that appeared during that time. These include Dead Piro Days, One Shot Episodes, hiccups and even (shudder) Shirt Guy Dom strips. For extra material I've added an "Endgames" short story complete with new drawings of Pirogoeth and the gameworld Largo.

If none of that made any sense to you and this is tne first time you've ever heard of "Megatokyo," I suppose an explanation of some sort is in order.

Megatokyo is an online webcomic that Rodney (Largo) and I (Piro) started back in August 2001. It is the story of Piro and Largo, two friends who fly to Japan on a whim and find themselves stranded, unable to afford the trip home.

New comics are posted every Monday, Wednesday, and Friday (usually) and each installment is (supposedly) designed to stand on it's own. When collected together, the intent is that they read as a cohesive story.

That's the idea, at any rate.

Since *Megatokyo* started, the website has grown a sizeable readership and has become home to a fairly active fan community. It's hard to grasp just how many people read and post to the *Megatokyo* site everyday, but it requires two dedicated servers (poor, overworked Makoto and Nayuki), will soon require a third, and bandwidth bills like this are kinda hard to ignore ^^;;

MT_vol_2_fr33talk.txt

Why does Volume 2 start with Chapter 1? Well, we weren't exactly organized when *Megatokyo* started. Development was literally no more than two or three random sketches before starting the first comic. Many things have changed and evolved since then, but the most significant change was going from a square, four-panel format to the manga-style format I use today. Around that time I started to organize things into chapters. The first 133 comics became "Chapter 0" and then I moved forward with "Chapter 1."

Let me recap the story so far:

After finding themselves unable to gain access to E3 Expo, Piro and Largo fly to Japan on a whim. After maxing out their credit cards on a shopping spree, they find that neither of them can afford tickets home (why did they buy one-way tickets in the first place? I have no clue).

They hook up with Piro's friend in Tokyo, Tsubasa, who gladly puts them up in his apartment while they try to figure out what to do next. Six weeks later, it becomes obvious that Tsubsasa is getting exasperated with them. Largo blackmails his friends Dom and Ed back home for some money, but unfortunately they spend it before they are able to buy plane tickets. Tsubasa is not amused by this.

Depressed, Piro goes to a bookstore where he reads all of the "girl's" manga he can find in a search for something that will help him figure out what to do. He has a run in with a plucky Japanese schoolgirl named Yuki and her friends, and in his flight leaves his bookbag behind.

Piro's conscience starts to bother him about all of this, so much so that she actually materializes as Seraphim, a tough talking little winged conscience. She tells him that he needs to take charge of the situation, get a job, and start earning the money to get home.

MT_vol_2_fr33talk.txt

While coming to terms with all of this, Piro almost haphazardly gives his railcard to a girl at a train station who appears flustered and upset about being late for an audition. He walks away without waiting for her to say thanks.

Largo, while wandering around Tokyo and guided by his conscience (a hamster named Boo) finds an Ancient Cave of Evil. He awakens what he believes is the Queen of Zombies -- a darkly cute girl who seems to take an unusual interest in him.

Piro manages to accidentally get a job at an anime store called "Megagamers" when Erika, the sexy bombshell who works there mistakes Piro for the new store mascot. Later, Erika's roommate Kimiko arrives and recognizes Piro (as he leaves the store) as the young man who gave her the railcard earlier that day.

Later that evening, Piro and Largo return to Tsubasa's apartment to find it empty. Upon the advice of Ping-chan, an experimental Emotional Doll System Accessory for the PS2, Tsubasa has sold his belongings and gone on a search for his childhood love. Piro and Largo are now homeless in Tokyo.

--

Not a very good synopsis, but it should give you the general idea. The best way to catch up on Chapter 0 is to read it -- either pick up volume one, or go online and read it there. Every *Megatokyo* comic, including the ones found in this book, you can read on the web. In fact, once you finish this book, if you want to see what happens next, head over to the website to pick up where this book leaves off:

http://www.megatokyo.com

Thanks for reading, and I hope you enjoy this volume. :)

Piro

メガトーキョー
megatokyo®
<OH, ERIKA? WHO'S THE NEW GUY, THE ONE IN THE PUCHIKO HAT?>
<I THINK I'VE SEEN HIM BEFORE.>
chapter 1:
"Do you want to save before you quit?"

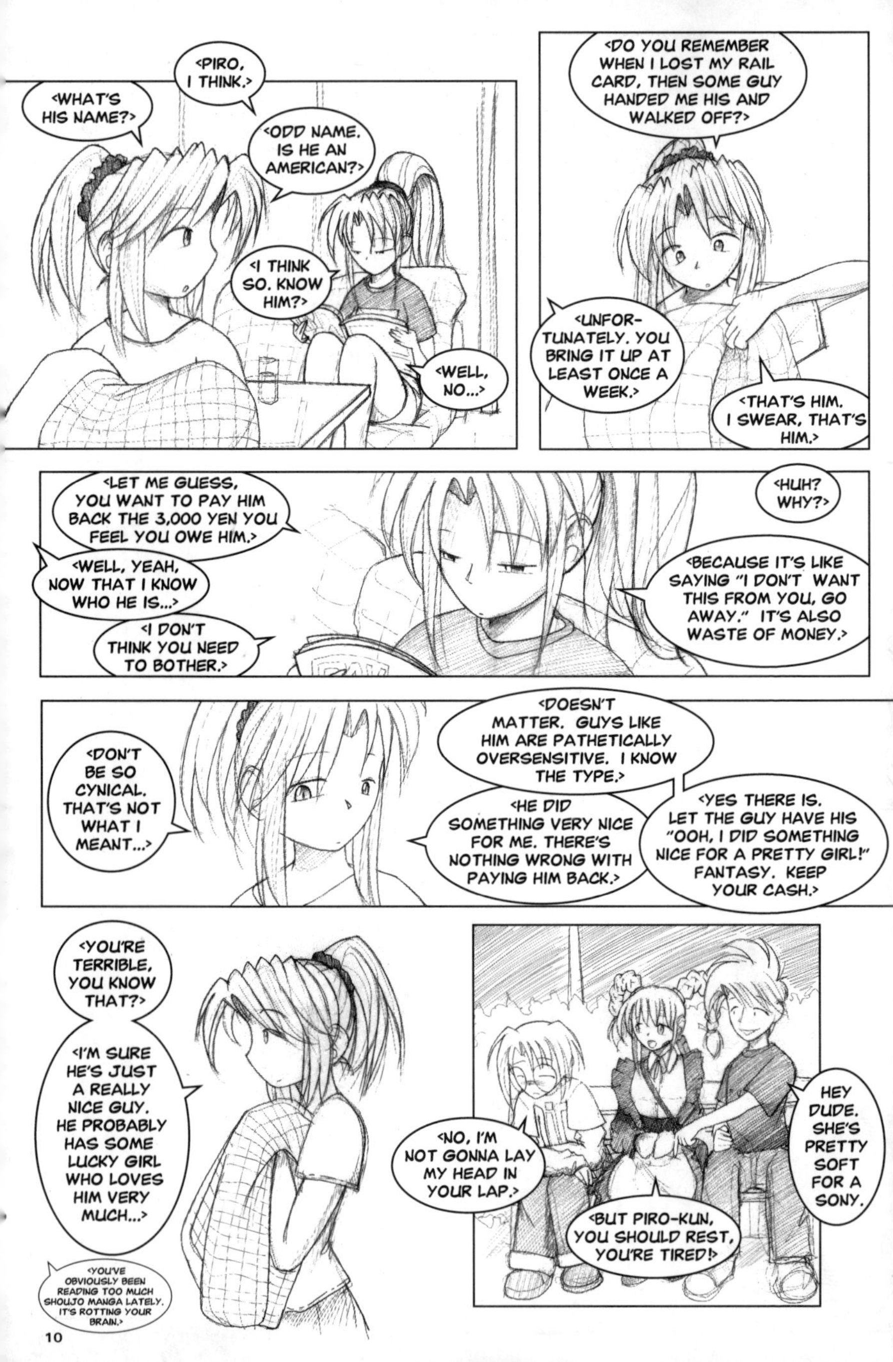

<WHAT'S HIS NAME?>
<PIRO, I THINK.>
<ODD NAME. IS HE AN AMERICAN?>
<I THINK SO. KNOW HIM?>
<WELL, NO...>
<DO YOU REMEMBER WHEN I LOST MY RAIL CARD, THEN SOME GUY HANDED ME HIS AND WALKED OFF?>
<UNFOR-TUNATELY. YOU BRING IT UP AT LEAST ONCE A WEEK.>
<THAT'S HIM. I SWEAR, THAT'S HIM.>
<LET ME GUESS, YOU WANT TO PAY HIM BACK THE 3,000 YEN YOU FEEL YOU OWE HIM.>
<WELL, YEAH, NOW THAT I KNOW WHO HE IS...>
<I DON'T THINK YOU NEED TO BOTHER.>
<HUH? WHY?>
<BECAUSE IT'S LIKE SAYING "I DON'T WANT THIS FROM YOU, GO AWAY." IT'S ALSO WASTE OF MONEY.>
<DON'T BE SO CYNICAL. THAT'S NOT WHAT I MEANT...>
<DOESN'T MATTER. GUYS LIKE HIM ARE PATHETICALLY OVERSENSITIVE. I KNOW THE TYPE.>
<HE DID SOMETHING VERY NICE FOR ME. THERE'S NOTHING WRONG WITH PAYING HIM BACK.>
<YES THERE IS. LET THE GUY HAVE HIS "OOH, I DID SOMETHING NICE FOR A PRETTY GIRL!" FANTASY. KEEP YOUR CASH.>
<YOU'RE TERRIBLE, YOU KNOW THAT?>
<I'M SURE HE'S JUST A REALLY NICE GUY. HE PROBABLY HAS SOME LUCKY GIRL WHO LOVES HIM VERY MUCH...>
<YOU'VE OBVIOUSLY BEEN READING TOO MUCH SHOUJO MANGA LATELY. IT'S ROTTING YOUR BRAIN.>
HEY DUDE. SHE'S PRETTY SOFT FOR A SONY.
<NO, I'M NOT GONNA LAY MY HEAD IN YOUR LAP.>
<BUT PIRO-KUN, YOU SHOULD REST, YOU'RE TIRED!>

WELL, NOW WHAT?
I DUNNO, I'M THINKING.
YOU DO THAT TOO MUCH.
LEAVE ME ALONE. I DON'T SEE YOU HAVING ANY IDEAS.
WE NEED BOOZE. AND FOOD. AND A FIRE. DEFINITELY A FIRE.
IF YOU HAVEN'T NOTICED, WE DON'T HAVE ANY MONEY.
FIR3 IS FR33.
LARGO, THIS ISN'T A CAMP-GROUND.
<UHM, PIRO-KUN.>
I SHALL SEEK THINGS THAT BURN.
NO! WE HAVE ENOUGH PROBLEMS!
<PIRO-KUN?>
<WHAT'S WRONG?>
<MY... BATTERIES ARE GETTING LOW. I NEED A POWER OUTLET.>
<UGH...>
LARGO, WE NEED TO FIND A POWER OUTLET. PING NEEDS TO RECHARGE.
POWER?
POWER...
THERE IS POWER...
ALL AROUND US.
WHUMP!
I CAN'T FIND YOUR OTHER SHOE. THIS ONE WAS THREE BLOCKS AWAY.
DOUMO ARIGATOU GOZAIMASU, LARGO-SAMA!!
I... H4V3... D4 POW3R..! PH33R...

I'M GOING TO WORK. DON'T DO ANYTHING STUPID WHILE I'M GONE. I CAN'T TAKE PING WITH ME, SO YOU'LL HAVE TO WATCH HER.
GANBATTE NE, PIRO-KUN!
SURE, WHATEVER.
I MUST DEAL WITH SOME UNFINISHED BUSINESS...
LARGO-SAMA~!
FUXØR
ZOMBIES STILL RUN RAMPANT THROUGHOUT THE CITY.
LARGO-SAMA~!
FUXØR
I WILL NOT TOLERATE THIS! I MUST ACT!
LARGO-SAMA~!
FUXØR
BEGONE! YOU ANNOYING CREATION OF THE EVIL EMPIRE!
LARGO-SAMA... HIDOI... HIDOI DESU..
<YOU KNOW HOW WE NEVER FINISHED THE ALGORITHMS THAT CONTROL HOW PING-E.D.S. UNITS DEAL WITH 'REJECTION'?>
<I JUST RAN A SIMULATION, LOOK.>
SONY
<OH WOW. CAN IT REALLY DO THAT?>
SONY
<LIFT AND THROW BUSSES? YEAH, I THINK THEY CAN.>

-BLINK-
-BLINK-
<OI. WAKE UP.>
<SORRY! SORRY, JUST... TIRED...>
<YOU LOOK LIKE HELL. TRY SLEEPING SOMETIME. IT'S GOOD FOR YOU.>
<I DID! I MEAN, I TRIED.>
MG
<MY FRIEND HERE IN TOKYO HAD TO LEAVE TOWN, SO NOW LARGO AND I DON'T HAVE ANYWHERE TO STAY.>
<WE SPENT THE NIGHT IN A PARK, BUT I NEED TO FIND A PLACE FOR US TO STAY.>
<I DON'T EVEN KNOW WHERE TO START...>
<WELL, THE STORE ROOM ON THE THIRD FLOOR USED TO BE AN APARTMENT.>
<IT'S A DUMP, BUT IT'S BETTER THAN SLEEPING IN THE PARK.>
<BUT... THE BOSS ISN'T GONNA LET US STAY IN THE STORE ROOM.>
<I'M SURE HE WON'T MIND.>
<SURE I WOULDN'T MIND WHAT?>
<DON'T LOOK AT ME LIKE THAT, HAYASAKA. IT GIVES ME THE SHIVERS.>
<BOSS, YOUR CIGARETTE...>

HUF
HUF
HUF
HUF
FUXOR
NYOW?
CRASH!
WHAT WOULD CAUSE ONE OF THOSE ANDROIDS TO BECOME HOMI-CIDAL?
DID SONY BUILD IN SOME SECRET FLAW?
HAVE I STUMBLED UPON IT'S SECRET PROGRAM-MING?
LARGO-SAMA!
DOKO ICCHATTA KASHIRA?
EEP...
THIS IS NOT GOOD.
LARGO-SAMA!
IT'S PIRO'S TOY. WHY IS IT TRYING TO KILL **ME**?
I'VE GOT BETTER THINGS TO DO THAN...
WOAH. STRONG 3VIL AURA
CLOSE...
IT'S THE QUEEN OF THE ZOMBIES!
WHY IS SHE DRESSED IN ONE OF THOSE SCHOOL UNIFORMS?
I SEE...
SHE'S HUNTING.
SEEKING FRESH BLOOD.
I WILL FOLLOW HER.
BUT I NEED...
...A DISGUISE.

私立大東
SHIRITSU DAITOU HIGH SCHOOL
<OHHH... WHO IS THAT?>
OH. IT'S YOU AGAIN.
ARE YOU FOLLOWING ME?
SHHH...
YOU CAN'T FOOL ME. I KNOW WHAT YOU ARE.
YOU PREY ON THE YOUNG BLOOD AT THIS SCHOOL.
HMM? INTERESTING OBSERVATION.
AND JUST WHAT ARE YOU SUPPOSED TO BE? "MIAMI VICE"?
HERE TO SAVE YOUNG GIRLS FROM FATES WORSE THAN DEATH?
HAHHHAAHHA! QU4K3 WITH PH34R, EVIL ONE! I AM NONE OTHER THAN...
AH! SENSEI! YOU MUST BE THE NEW ENGLISH TEACHER! WELCOME TO SHIRITSU DAITOU HIGH SCHOOL!

<WELL, YOU AREN'T RUNNING A TEMPERATURE, BUT I CALLED THE SCHOOL ANYWAY. NOW EAT SOME BREAKFAST BEFORE IT GETS COLD.>

<I'M NOT HUNGRY.>

<YUKI! YOU SHOULD EAT SOMETHING!>
<WHAT'S WRONG WITH THAT GIRL TODAY?>
<NO IDEA.>

<I FEEL SICK.>
<I'M SO NERVOUS.>

<I WONDER IF HE'S MAD AT ME? I DIDN'T REALLY DO ANYTHING WRONG.>
<THAT'S NOT IT THOUGH... I JUST... I JUST WANT TO ASK HIM... BUT I CAN'T.>

<HE'LL JUST SAY I'M A STUPID GIRL, AND TELL ME TO GO AWAY.>

<MAYBE...>

<IF I WASN'T SO UGLY AND SO PLAIN...>
<HE'D SAY "YES.">

<LARGO-SAMA! WHERE ARE YOU?>

<LARGO-SAMA...>
KLANG!
KLANG!!

<WHAT SHOULD I DO? I HAVE TO FIND LARGO-SAMA AND THEN...>

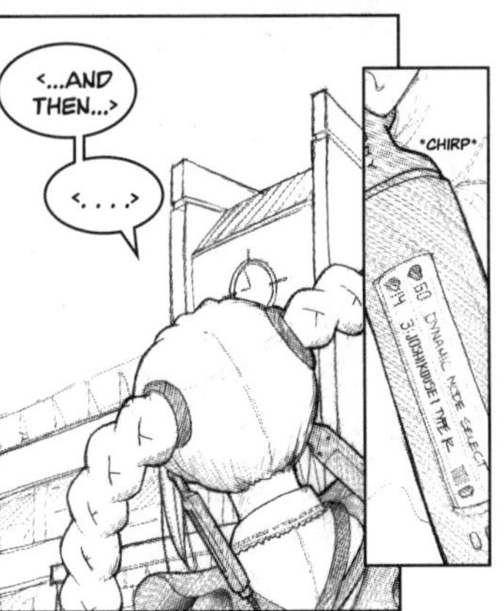
<...AND THEN...>
<. . . .>
CHIRP
60 DYNAMIC MODE SELECT
14 3:JOSHIKOUSEI TYPE R

WE WERE NOT EXPECTING YOU UNTIL TOMORROW, BUT YOU ARE WELCOME TO START. PLEASE EXCUSE MY ENGLISH, IT IS NOT VERY GOOD.

WHAT LUCK! THIS GUY THINKS I'M THIS NEW TEACHER!
THIS IS THE PERFECT COVER FOR ME!

NOW I CAN FIND OUT JUST HOW DEEPLY HER UNDEAD ARMY HAS INFILTRATED THIS SCHOOL.
OR AT THE VERY LEAST I CAN USE THE SCHOOL'S COMPUTER LAB TO PLAY SOME QUAKE...

PH33R NOT. I WILL TEACH THEM WELL.
<OHH! HE IS USING VERY DYNAMIC ENGLISH PHRASES!>
<OHH... EXCELLENT!>

HMM HM HMM!! :)
<WHERE DID THIS THING COME FROM? WHERE'S MY UNIFORM?>

<CLASS, I WOULD LIKE TO INTRODUCE YOU TO YOUR NEW ENGLISH TEACHER, LARGO-SENSEI. LET US GIVE HIM A WARM WEL-COME!>

** hushed silence **

TAK
TAK
TAK
TIC
TAK
TAK
TAK
TAK
ZAK
TAK
TIC
TIC
TACK

I AM **GREAT TEACHER LARGO!!!!**
PH33R MY L33T T34CHING SKI||Z!
RULZ.
NO CAMPING
NO ZOMBIEZ

WHY? WHY LEARN? WHY SUBMIT YOURSELF TO GREAT TEACHER LARGO?? WHAT IS IN IT FOR YOU?
I WILL TELL YOU...

BECAUSE KNOWL3DG3 IS POW3R!!

WE SHALL ROCK THE FOUNDATIONS OF THIS SCHOOL WITH THAT POWER!
NOW SAY IT!
EEP!
NO-RAGE... IZ...
POWAA...

AGAIN!!
NO-RAGE... IZ...
POWAA...
AGAIN!!
<I'M HUNGRY...>

YES CLASS, VERY GOOD. VERY GOOD.
LARGO-SENSEI!!!!
OH NO! THAT INSANE PS2 ACCESSORY IS...
IN MY CLASS??
<LARGO-SENSEI!! I'M SORRY I'M LATE!!>
THIS... IS NOT GOOD...
I AM... SURROUNDED.
THEY ARE EVERYWHERE.
EVIL, ALL AROUND ME...
WALLS CLOSING IN, CAN'T BREATHE!
MUST...
ESCAPE!!
<OOHHHHH!>
<I THINK HE BROKE HIS LEG.>
<NO, WAIT! HE'S STAGGERING AWAY!!>
<YAY! GO GO, GREAT TEACHER LARGO!!>
<IT SEEMS THAT YOU KNOW EACH OTHER.>
<HOW... INTRIGUING.>
<LARGO-SENSEI...>

WHAT A JERK! NAKAJIMA SHOULD GET RUN OVER BY A GARBAGE TRUCK. WHAT A MEAN THING TO SAY! I JUST CAN'T UNDERSTAND WHY YUMI LIKES THAT IDIOT.
なかよし
SHE FINDS HIS POCKET COMPUTER IN THE GRASS, GETS HERSELF ALL WORKED UP ABOUT RETURNING IT TO HIM, EVEN BUYS BATTERIES FOR IT... AND THEN HE JUST BLOWS HER OFF WHEN SHE RETURNS IT! WHAT A HEARTLESS BASTARD!
<UHM...>
<EXCUSE ME...>
<MR. PIRO-SAN?>
<I FOUND YOUR BOOKBAG A FEW WEEKS AGO, AND I DIDN'T KNOW HOW TO GET IT BACK TO YOU...>
<I SAW THAT YOU WORKED HERE AND...>
<I'M SORRY! I'M SO SORRY!!>
<I TRIED TO EMAIL YOU, BUT YOU NEVER RESPONDED, AND THEN I... I...>
<I'M SORRY! PLEASE TAKE IT!!>
WHAT DO I DO? WHAT DO I...
ACK, I CAN'T DO THAT...
<I WOULD HAVE RETURNED IT SOONER, BUT I DIDN'T KNOW WHERE TO FIND YOU...>
<AND... AND I...>
UHH...

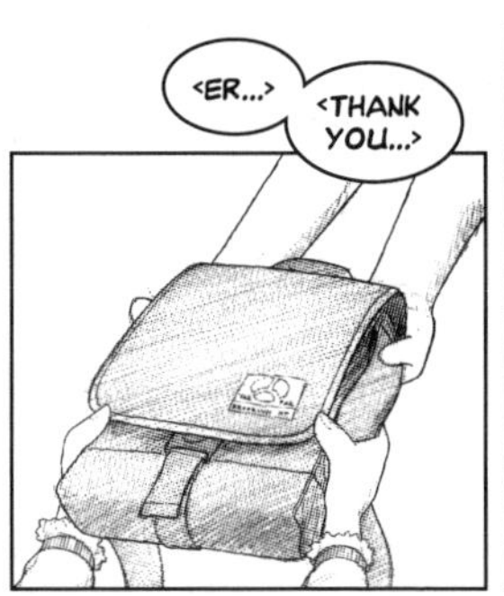
<ER...>
<THANK YOU...>

I GOTTA SAY SOMETHIN... WHAT THOUGH? THINKTHINK THINK...

OH! I GOT IT! I THINK...
<UHM, I...>
<I KNOW YOUR SKETCHBOOK HAS TO BE VERY IMPORTANT TO YOU, AND IT MUST HAVE UPSET YOU VERY MUCH TO HAVE LOST IT. I'M SORRY, I SHOULD HAVE...>
<I SHOULD HAVE...>

OHMYGOD THE SKETCHBOOK...
<EHEHEHEH, OH THAT THING? IT'S JUST FULL OF CRAPPY DOODLES. I... HOPE YOU DIDN'T WASTE YOUR TIME LOOKING THROUGH IT, I MEAN, YOU COULDA JUST TOSSED **THAT** OLD THING, HEH, EHEHEH, HEH...>

<WHAT??? HOW COULD YOU SAY THAT? YOUR ART IS BEAUTIFUL! IT'S AMAZING! IT WOULD BE A HORRIBLE CRIME TO-->
<YUKI-CHAN?>

<YUKI-CHAN! WHAT ARE YOU DOING HERE? WHY WEREN'T YOU IN SCHOOL TODAY?>
<TSK TSK, SKIPPIN CLASSES. THAT'S A FIRST. SO, WHAT'S UP, LITTLE MISS PERFECT?>

<ACTUALLY, WHAT ARE YOU DOING? PLANNING ON DITCHING US TODAY?>
<WERE YOU SICK THIS MORNING? ARE YOU FEELING BETTER NOW?>
<YOU LOOK LIKE YOU'RE FEELING BETTER.>
<HEY, ISN'T THAT THE GUY YOU STOLE THE BOOKBAG FROM? THE ONE FROM THE BOOK-STORE?>
UWAHEEEE~???
<HAHAHAH, NONONO, I DIDN'T STEAL ANYTHING I, I WAS JUST...>
<OI, PIRO, HERE'S YOUR LUNCH. I'M TIRED OF WATCHING YOU...>
<...STARVE. WELL, WELL, WHAT'S THIS?>
<MAKING SOME NEW FRIENDS?>
UWA...
<I...>
<MR. PIRO-SAN, I AM VERY SORRY ABOUT THE DELAY IN RETURNING YOUR SKETCHBOOK. I AM GLAD THAT I WAS ABLE TO RETURN IT. THANK YOU, PLEASE HAVE A NICE AFTER-NOON.>
<LETS GO, MAMI-CHAN, ASAKO.>
<YUKI-CHAN?>
<HINT: NEXT TIME, HIT ON THEM WHEN THEIR FRIENDS AREN'T AROUND.>
<BUT, I DIDN'T...>

<HEY, WAIT UP! WHAT WAS THAT ALL ABOUT?>
<YUKI-CHAN, WHAT'S WRONG?>
<NOTHING.>
<YOU LOOK UPSET!>
<I SAID IT'S NOTHING.>
<DIDN'T LOOK LIKE NOTHING. COME ON, GIVE.>
<IT'S NONE OF YOUR BUSINESS.>
OF ALL THE YOUNG MEN IN TOKYO SHE HAS TO PICK MY CLIENT.
I DON'T LIVE RIGHT.
THAT LITTLE GIRL HAS GOT WAY TOO MUCH PLUCK FOR MY COMFORT. PIRO HAS TROUBLE DEALING WITH THE BASICS, NEVERMIND THIS. I REALLY NEED TO PUT A STOP TO...
WHAT THE...
HAVE YOU SEEN
I REALLY HOPE WE'RE NOT PAYING HIM.
MAYBE I'LL GET LUCKY AND SOMEONE WILL STEP ON HIM.

HAVE YOU SEEN
SQUEEK!
IS... THAT YOU, LITTLE DUDE? I'M... DONE FOR. THE DARKNESS, IT'S... BEAUTIFUL...
SQUEE, SQUEEK SQUE3K, SQUE4K...
SQU333K!!
1¥·ARCADE
アーケード
WHOOSH!
POW!
SQU34K!!!
SOMETHING.... CALLING ME BACK...
A LIGHT... I SEE...
A BRIGHT... LIGHT...
SHINING...
SQUEEK!
NO, I WILL NOT LEND YOU SOME QUART- ERS.

<I DON'T KNOW WHY YOU ARE BEING SO NICE TO ME, TOHYA-SAN. DO YOU THINK WE CAN BE FRIENDS?>
<I DON'T SEE WHY NOT...>
<YOU ARE...>
<RATHER INTERES-TING.>
<WAI~! THAT MAKES ME FEEL VERY HAPPY!>
<SO, PING-SAN, WHERE DO YOU LIVE AGAIN?>
<WHERE DO I LIVE?>
<THAT'S ODD. I DON'T ACTUALLY KNOW WHERE I LIVE.>
<HOW VERY STRANGE.>
<LET ME THINK...>
<WE DON'T LIVE IN THE PARK... PIRO-KUN SAID HE WAS GOING TO WORK... I KNOW WHERE PIRO-KUN WORKS. MAYBE I CAN FIND PIRO-KUN AT WORK? I THINK.>
<PIRO-KUN... IS THIS YOUR "BOY-FRIEND"?>
<WAHH! DON'T SAY THAT SO PLAINLY!! ITS EMBAR-RASING!!>
<I MEAN, ER, MAYBE.. HE MIGHT BE MY BROTHER, OR MAYBE MY COUSIN... OR A CHILDHOOD FRIEND? I DON'T REALLY KNOW YET...>
<YOU DON'T KNOW?>
<I'M SORRY, BUT PIRO-KUN HASN'T PLAYED WITH ME ENOUGH FOR ME TO KNOW WHAT OUR RELATIONSHIP IS. MY PERSONALITY CONSTRUCTS ARE LIMITED UNTIL WE PLAY A FEW GAMES AND HE MAKES SOME SELECTIONS. I'M WORKING WITH VERY LIMITED DATA.>
<AMAZING. YOU REALLY ARE ONE OF THOSE PS2 ROBOT-GIRLS. I'D HEARD RUMORS, BUT I DIDN'T KNOW THAT ANY ACTUALLY EXISTED.>
<UH HUH. I'M A SONY SEVS 44936 EDS, JUST A PROTO-TYPE, ACTUALLY.>
<UHM... IS THAT OK? IF IT'S NOT, I'LL GO AWAY. SOME PEOPLE DON'T LIKE ROBOTS...>
<ACTUALLY, I SUDDENLY HAVE RENEWED FAITH IN THE PS2 PLATFORM.>
<YOU THINK SO? I THINK IT'S LIKE AN IRRITATING, ANNOYING WHINY LITTLE BROTHER.>

<WILL YOU PLEASE LEAVE ME ALONE?? WHERE DO YOU GET THESE STUPID IDEAS.>
<ALL I DID WAS RETURN HIS BOOKBAG, END OF DISCUSSION. THERE IS NOTHING ELSE. NOTHING.>

BOO...
I FEEL...
ALIVE AGAIN...
THIS PLACE...
SQUEEK!
I'VE BEEN AWAY FROM IT ALL TOO LONG.
I NEED QUARTERS...
I NEED TO PLAY...
I MUST PLAY...
HMMM....
YOU'RE A LOT LIKE A VAMPIRE YOURSELF, AREN'T YOU?
YOU FEED OFF HE STIMULATION AND THE RUSH OF VIDEO GAMES.
YOU CANNOT LIVE WITHOUT IT.
WITHOUT IT, YOU ARE NOTHING BUT AN EMPTY SHELL.
DON'T EVEN TRY TO APPLY YOUR UNDEAD VIEWS ON ME.
VIDEO GAMES ARE A CONDUIT FOR THE SOUL.
THEY EXPAND OUR LIVES, CHANNEL OUR IMAGINA-TION, TEST OUR SKILLZ.
GAMES EXIST AS A CHANNEL FOR THE BOUNDLESS ENERGY OF PEOPLE ALL OVER THE WORLD.
IT IS A MEDIUM YOU ARE INCAPABLE OF UNDER-STANDING.
IS THAT WHAT YOU THINK?
ONE COULD SAY THAT ABOUT MANY THINGS WE "NEED."
YET SUCH NEEDS USUALLY ENTAIL... AN EXCHANGE.
SUCH AS THESE.
THEY ARE REQUIRED TO PLAY.
PERHAPS... A CHALLENGE IS IN ORDER?
YOU? CHALLENGE ME? HAHHA! I'LL DISPATCH YOU BACK TO THE DARKNESS FROM WHENCE YOU CAME!
CHEH. I WASN'T THINKING ABOUT ME...
<TOHYA-SAN, THERE YOU ARE!>

WHERE IN THE WORLD DID SHE COME FROM?
AND WHY DID SHE HAVE MY BOOKBAG?
THAT WASN'T THE SAME GIRL... WAS IT?
NO... DIFFERENT GIRL.
IT'S DEFINITELY MY BOOKBAG. EVERYTHING IS HERE.
I WONDER WHY SHE GOT SO WORKED UP OVER THE SKETCHBOOK?
I CAN'T BELIEVE SHE LOOKED THROUGH IT. HOW EMBARRASSING. NONE OF THIS STUFF WAS EVER SUPPOSED TO BE SEEN BY...
ANYONE...
ELSE...
WHAT THE...
<I don't think you could tie a ribbon in your hair like this.>
<Hair clips would help.>
SHE... WROTE... COMMENTS... ON THEM??
ON... EVERY PAGE??
<the demi bra is very cute, but it looks uncomfortable.>
<is this why she looks so sad?>
<SHE'S RIGHT, YOU KNOW, THOUGH I DOUBT SHE SPEAKS FROM PERSONAL EXPERIENCE.>
<I'M HEADING HOME. HELP THE BOSS CLOSE UP.>
FWAP!

SO, DO YOU ACCEPT THE CHALLENGE?
I WANT TO KNOW IF IT IS HOT AIR OR BLOOD THAT RUNS THRU YOUR VEINS.
<TOHYA-SAN, PEOPLE ARE STARING AT US. WHAT ARE YOU DOING?>
POOR CHOICE OF WORDS, COMING FROM YOU.
I ACCEPT THE CHALLENGE, BUT I WILL NOT PLAY AGAINST YOUR MINION.
I AM YOUR DOOM.
YOUR TAUNTS ARE GETTING OLD. DEFEAT PING AND WE SHALL SEE.
PROVE TO ME YOU ARE WORTHY COMPETITION.
NOW, CHOOSE YOUR GAME.
CHOOSE WISELY.
HA! THAT'S EASY.
I CHOOSE...
JO! C|-|IL.
wait!
C4R3PHUL |]UD3, |]ON7 L3T H3R +RIC|< YOU. J00 90++@ CHOO$3 +H3 RI9H+ 94M3, OR 5H3 WILL OWNZOR YOU.
WHO THE...?
careful, my brother. beware of her trickery. you must chooseth the correct game, or your defeat is inevitable
J00 5@ M4 45$, M4N. |]U|\3, NOW IT'S MY 7URN 70 R3+URN T3H PH@VOR.
you saved my life, and now i will do the same for you.

<OI.>
<WELCOME HOME! HOW WAS WORK?>
<ENTERTAINING. YOUR GENEROUS ADMIRER WAS LIVING IN INOKASHIRA PARK.>
<REEHHHHHH?? HE WHAT??>
<SEEMS HIS FRIEND GOT TIRED OF SUPPORTING HIM AND TOSSED HIM OUT.>
<THAT'S TERRIBLE! WE HAVE TO DO SOMETHING!>
<RELAX. THE BOSS IS LETTING HIM STAY IN THE APARTMENT OVER THE STORE.>
<YOU LOOK TIRED. YOU EATEN YET?>
<HUH? ER, NO, NOT YET.>
<YOU HAVEN'T BEEN EATING ANY OF THE GROCERIES I'VE BEEN BUYING LATELY.>
<WHAT'S WITH THE DIET?>
<YOU'RE ALREADY TOO SCRAWNY.>
<I'M NOT. I'VE... JUST BEEN EATING ON THE RUN A LOT...>
<YOU LOOK LIKE HELL. IT'S STARTING TO SHOW IN YOUR FACE.>
<YOUR LOOKS ARE AN IMPORTANT ASSET, NANASAWA.>
<DON'T MESS WITH THEM.>
<THINK A VOICE ACTRESS GETS BY ON JUST HER VOICE? YOU DON'T PUT OUT ENOUGH TO GET BY WITHOUT BEING PRETTY TOO.>
<I'M GOING TO WORK! GOODBYE!>
<HMPH!>
<WHAT'S HER PROBLEM?>
<I DO **NOT** LOOK "SCRAWNY.">
<DO I?>
<MAYBE I CAN GET SOMETHING AT THE RESTAURANT.>
<I SHOULD EAT, BUT I DON'T GET PAID TILL TOMORROW.>
<ERIKA DOESN'T UNDERSTAND.>
<I CAN'T LET HER PAY FOR EVERYTHING ANYMORE.>
<I HAVE TO SUPPORT MYSELF.>
<I JUST WISH SHE'D LET ME.>

YOU LOOK FAMILIAR...
LOO|< O|_|T, DOOD. T|-|15 <|-|IXOR CO|_|LD ROX3R JOOR BOX3RZ 4T |\|3 LL4|\/|4Z G4|\/|3
T|-|3Z3 .JP |<IDD|3Z |\/|4Y LOO|< I|\|OC3|\|7, 8|_|7 T|-|3Y'R3 7RYI|\|G 2 FOOL JOO
beware, there may be treachery afoot. do not underestimate these asian females.
I WILL NOT LOSE. I DON'T CARE IF IT'S GOT MAD SKILLZ OR NOT.
I WILL NOT BACK DOWN.
DOOD, I DID|\|7 54Y |<\/\/17
PIC|< JOOR G4|\/|3 \/\/IZ3LY
comrade, you need not abandon the field of battle.
just choose your battlefield carefully.
PL4Y3R 2 IZ 4 L177L3 G|_|RL.
you must know your enemies weaknesses...
|_|53 JOOR 5|<ILLZ *4|\|D* JOOR 57R3|\|G7|-| 2G37|-|3R 2 |\/|4|<3 |-|3R \/\/33P
MOSH MOSH REVOLUTION!
MOSH!
...as well as your own strengths.
"MOSH MOSH REVOLUTION?"
YEA, IT'S LIKE "DANCE DANCE REVOLUTION" IN A MOSHPIT WITH PUNK MUSIC.
IT ROX.
<TOHYA-SAN, WHAT'S A "MOSH"?>
SW33T!!

A LAME, BUT SOMEHOW APPRO-PRIATE CHOICE.
SHALL WE CONTINUE?
<LARGO-SAN, WHAT'S GOING ON?>
PH34R! IT BEGINS...
KONAMI
KONAMI
WOOT!!
<TOHYA-SAN...>
<KAY>
<JUST FOLLOW THE PATTERNS ON THE SCREEN, PING-CHAN. IT'S NOT VERY DIFFICULT.>
MMR
NSTOP MEGAMOS
BATTLE MODE!!!
ME YOUR BEST MOSH
W ME YOUR MOVES!
VICTORY WILL BE MIN3...
READY, SET...
THERE IT GOES AGAIN.
THE LIGHTS KEEP FLICKERING ON AND OFF.
I WONDER WHAT THE...
<UHM, BOSS? IS THERE A GAME CENTER OR ARCADE SOMEWHERE IN THIS POWER GRID?>

<HEY, WHAT'S GOIN ON?>
<SOME KINDA CHALLENGE ON THE MOSH MOSH REVOLUTION MACHINE.>
<WOW, LOOK AT THEM GO!>
<LET ME SEE!>
<I GOT HURT PLAYIN' THAT GAME LAST WEEK.>
<WHO'S THE GAIJIN?>
<HEY, ISN'T THAT...>
<IT'S GREAT TEACHER LARGO!!>
<AND THAT NEW GIRL!>
<AMAZING!>
<THEY'RE EVENLY MATCHED! NEITHER ONE HAS MISSED A MOVE!!>
<500 YEN ON THE GAIJIN!>
KONAMI
VERY DANGEROUS, YO!
<HEY...>
BATTERY LOW
AUTO MODE
POWERSAVE...
BEEP!
<DIDN'T GREAT TEACHER LARGO BREAK HIS LEG?>
KONAMI
<OH YEA!!>
KRACK
<WHEN HE JUMPED OUT THE WINDOW, RIGHT?>
KONAMI

SNAP!
WHAM!
CRUNCH
SNICK!
CRINKLE
FZZZZZZZZZZTTTT!!!!
<HEY! WHAT HAPPENED TO THE LIGHTS!
<EEEK!!!>
<HELP! HELP!>
<OWW! DON'T PUSH!>
<WHO WON? WHO WON?>
<I SMELL SMOKE!!>
SQUEEK!!
ABUNAI!!
<RUN! RUN!>
<WOO! RIOT! RIOT!>
<HELP! I HURT MY LEG!!>
<RUN FOR YOUR LIVES!!>
<HNNNG... STOP PUSH...>
<OOFFF! UHNN...>
WONDERFUL. A SMALL RIOT.
THIS MESS HAS "LARGO" WRITTEN ALL OVER IT.
CAN'T LEAVE THAT IDIOT OUT OF MY SIGHT FOR MORE THAN TEN MINUTES.
HE BETTER NOT HAVE LOST PING, I'LL KILL HIM.
5\//33T R|_|/\/ DOOD, 8|_|T |-|34/>5L4MMING T|-|3 5CR33N? B4D, DOOD. B4444D
HURT... BAD... MUST.. SHARE... P4IN...
excellent battle! next time, do not use suicidal finishing move.

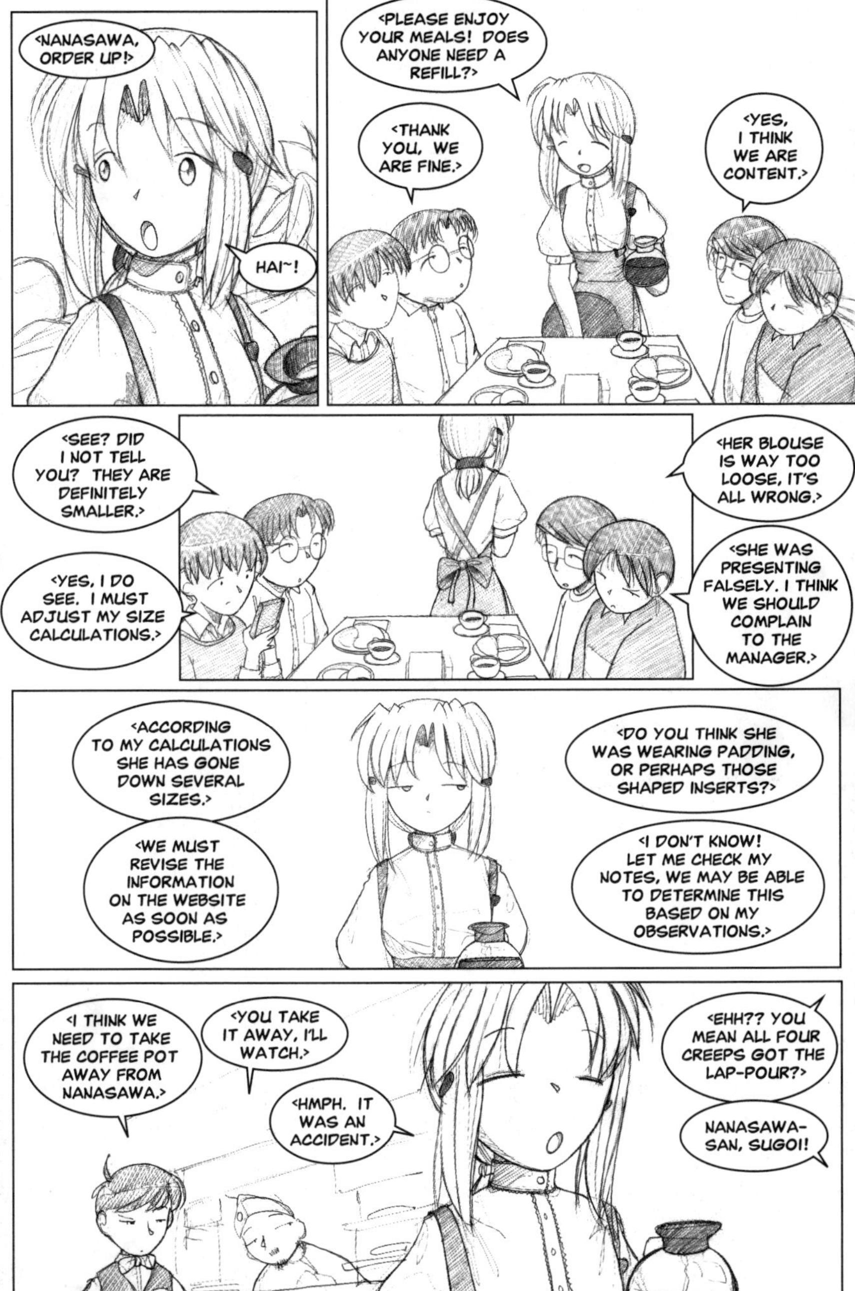
<NANASAWA, ORDER UP!>
HAI~!
<PLEASE ENJOY YOUR MEALS! DOES ANYONE NEED A REFILL?>
<THANK YOU, WE ARE FINE.>
<YES, I THINK WE ARE CONTENT.>
<SEE? DID I NOT TELL YOU? THEY ARE DEFINITELY SMALLER.>
<YES, I DO SEE. I MUST ADJUST MY SIZE CALCULATIONS.>
<HER BLOUSE IS WAY TOO LOOSE, IT'S ALL WRONG.>
<SHE WAS PRESENTING FALSELY. I THINK WE SHOULD COMPLAIN TO THE MANAGER.>
<ACCORDING TO MY CALCULATIONS SHE HAS GONE DOWN SEVERAL SIZES.>
<WE MUST REVISE THE INFORMATION ON THE WEBSITE AS SOON AS POSSIBLE.>
<DO YOU THINK SHE WAS WEARING PADDING, OR PERHAPS THOSE SHAPED INSERTS?>
<I DON'T KNOW! LET ME CHECK MY NOTES, WE MAY BE ABLE TO DETERMINE THIS BASED ON MY OBSERVATIONS.>
<I THINK WE NEED TO TAKE THE COFFEE POT AWAY FROM NANASAWA.>
<YOU TAKE IT AWAY, I'LL WATCH.>
<HMPH. IT WAS AN ACCIDENT.>
<EHH?? YOU MEAN ALL FOUR CREEPS GOT THE LAP-POUR?>
NANASAWA-SAN, SUGOI!

I SWEAR, ONE OF THESE DAYS I'M JUST GONNA LEAVE THE IDIOT TO...

YOU'RE...
"PIRO"?

ME? ER, UHM.. YES?
WHUMP

I SEE.

<I'LL COME BY AND PICK UP PING-CHAN FOR SCHOOL TOMOR-ROW.>
<DON'T FORGET TO PLUG HER IN, SHE HAD A LONG DAY.>
<GOOD NIGHT, PIRO-KUN.>

DO I... KNOW HER?
J0, SPID3Y. J00 D0|\|'7 G07 |\|0 P0\/\/3RZ, D4TS J00R |-|4IR SPARKIN
L33T SENSES TINGLING...
PIRO...
IN DANGER...
PH34R...
my super-hero friend, your hair is on fire.

<PING-CHAN? HELLO? COME ON, IT'S TIME TO GO HOME.>
LARGO, SHE'S COMPLETELY SHUT DOWN. WHAT HAPPENED?
WE CAN REBUILD HER!
NEVERMIND...
MOSH

WHERE'D THE SCHOOL UNIFORM COME FROM?
LOOKS LIKE SHIRITSU DAITOU SERAFUKU...
THE ZOMBIE QUEEN.
LEGIONS OF SYCOPHANTS TO PROTECT HER.
THESE TACTICS SEEM... FAMILIAR.

THIS...
PURE... EVIL...
I KNOW I'VE FELT IT BEFORE...
BUT WHERE?

OOF. SHE'S HEAVY.
COME ON. WE'VE GOT A PLACE TO STAY NOW.
WE DO?

DID YOU CHECK TO MAKE SURE IT'S ZOMBIE-PROOF?
DON'T I ALWAYS?

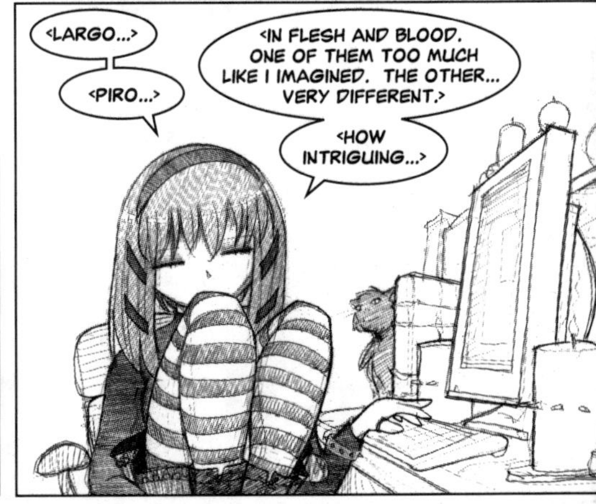
<LARGO...>
<PIRO...>
<IN FLESH AND BLOOD. ONE OF THEM TOO MUCH LIKE I IMAGINED. THE OTHER... VERY DIFFERENT.>
<HOW INTRIGUING...>

<SO, IS CUBE-SOFT STILL INTERESTED IN YOU FOR THAT PART?>
<IT SEEMS SO. THEY WANT ME TO COME AND DO A READING FOR THE CHARACTER TOMORROW.>

<YOU DON'T SOUND VERY THRILLED.>
<I'M NOT SURE I REALLY WANT THE PART. >

<NOT THIS AGAIN. YOU'RE CRAZY. I'D KILL FOR A ROLE LIKE THAT.>
<LET ME GUESS, YOU'LL PASS ON THE PART BECAUSE YOU DON'T LIKE THE WAY THESE GAMES TOY WITH THE EMOTIONS AND FEELINGS OF SHY, LONELY, GUYS.>
<OOTAKA-SAN, CAN I HAVE A SPAGHETTI DINNER TO GO?>
<YES MA'M>

<YOU THINK ITS WRONG TO LEAD THEM ON, PROMOTING THE FANTASY THAT YOUR CHARACTER ACTUALLY CARES FOR THEM.>
<THE WEIRD THING IS, YOU DO CARE, WHICH IS WHY YOU'LL TURN DOWN THE ROLE.>
<I THINK YOU'RE LOOKING AT IT ALL WRONG.>

<MAYBE A LITTLE FANTASY ISN'T ALWAYS SUCH A BAD THING.>
<MAYBE THERE ARE TIMES WHEN A GUY REALLY NEEDS IT, WHEN HE'S REALLY DOWN.>
<MAYBE THEN IT'S A GOOD THING.>

<OOTAKA-SAN?>
<CAN YOU MAKE THAT TWO SPAGHETTI DINNERS TO GO?>

WELL, HERE IT IS.
HOME AWAY FROM HOME.
DID YOU PICK UP SOME BEER?
NO.
IT IS NOT "HOME" IF THERE IS NO BEER.
FINE. YOU CAN SLEEP IN THE PARK.
THE PARK OFFERS POOR DEFENSES.
I MUST SECURE THE PERIMETER.
WHATEVER MAKES YOU HAPPY.
NOW, I JUST NEED TO FIND AN OUTLET.
<GHAAAAA!!>
<WHA? WHERE AM I? WHAT...>
<YOUR BATTERIES DIED. YOU WERE IN SOME KIND OF SLEEP MODE.>
<A FEW HOURS PLUGGED IN AND YOU SHOULD BE FINE.>
<KYAA... I'M STILL IN MY UNIFORM. I HAVE TO CHANGE INTO APPROPRIATE CLOTHES.>
<UHMM... PIRO-ONIISAN...>
<I REALLY NEED TO CHANGE MY CLOTHES.>
<AND... YOU KNOW... A GIRL NEEDS A LITTLE... PRIVACY...>
LARGO, HAVE YOU EVER HAD A CONSOLE ACCESSORY TELL YOU TO "GET OUT" BEFORE?
ONLY THE WEIRD CRAP YOU PLAY. THAT'S WHY ALL GAMES SHOULD HAVE GUNS.

<THIS MUST BE IT.>
<I HOPE I'M NOT BEING TOO PRESUMP-TUOUS.>
<FROM WHAT ERIKA SAID, I THINK HE MIGHT APPRECIATE A GOOD MEAL.>
<BUT WHAT AM I GOING TO SAY?>
<"HI! YOU DON'T KNOW ME, BUT I BROUGHT YOU SOME DINNER!">
<"I GOT THIS FOR YOU BECAUSE I STILL OWE YOU FOR THAT RAIL-CARD.">
<THIS COULD BE AWKWARD.>
<PIRO-KUN! I THINK THERE'S SOMEONE AT THE DOOR!>
<HI~!>
<CAN I HELP YOU?>
CLOCKED
<DAMNIT PING, GET AWAY FROM THE DOOR.>
<STOP GOOFING AROUND, YOUR...>
CLOCKED
<OH!>
<ER... HELLO.>
<CAN I, ER, HELP YOU?>

<HELLO, MY NAME IS NANASAWA KIMIKO. NICE TO MEET YOU.>
<I'M HAYASAKA-SAN'S ROOMMATE.>
<ER, NICE TO... TO...>
<HAYASAKA-SAN'S... OH YEAH... IN THE STORE... YESTERDAY... YOU... AND... UH...>
<UHMM... ERIKA THOUGHT THAT I SHOULD BRING SOME FOOD BY FOR YOU... AND...>
<...YOUR FRIEND.>
<WELL, I MEAN, I WORK IN A RESTAURANT, AND... WITH YOU MOVING INTO A NEW APARTMENT AND EVERYTHING... AND...>
<AND...>
<OK! I HAVE TO GO NOW! IT WAS NICE MEETING YOU!>
<BYE NOW!>
<ERR...>
<THANK YOU...>
<...VERY MUCH...>
<BYE...>
EGAGAME
<WELL! I'M GLAD TO SEE HE'S DOING OK!>
<NOTHING TO WORRY ABOUT.>

<WAH! THIS PLACE IS SO MESSY!!>
HERE. HAYASAKA-SAN'S FRIEND BROUGHT US SOME FOOD.
ZOMBIE QUEEN...
I KNOW I'VE FELT THIS EVIL SOMEWHERE BEFORE...
BUT WHERE?
SW33T!! IT'S SPAGHETTI!!
WHERE WAS I? OH YEAH. THE EVIL. I REMEMBER NOW. THERE WAS A GREAT BATTLE...
I PH34R NOT YOUR FACELESS MINIONS!!
I AM YOUR DOOM!! FACE ME AND FEEL MY SWORD!!
...
YOU ARE NOT WORTHY OF EFFORT.
BEGONE.
OH CRAP.

DUDE, WE'VE GOT A SERIOUS PROBLEM.
3VIL L33T
"HELLO, MY NAME IS NANASAWA KIMIKO. NICE TO MEET YOU."
I JUST REALIZED WHO OUR ENEMY IS. DO YOU REMEMBER WHEN...
I HAVE TO SAY, MY HEART SKIPPED A BEAT. HER VOICE, HER EXPRESSION, HER SMILE.
BUT SUDDENLY, HER EXPRESSION CHANGED, JUST FOR A MOMENT. MAYBE I WASN'T SUPPOSED TO SEE...
AND THEN SHE WAS GONE. SHE SEEMED... SO... SAD. I WONDER...
GAH, WHAT AM I THINKING? THIS ISN'T A GAME.
HEH. I'M SUCH AN IDIOT.
BAKA.
...AND THAT'S WHY WE NEED TO FIND A STORE THAT SELLS ROCKET LAUNCHERS.
HELP ME WITH THIS PHONE BOOK.

<HEY, ERIKA...>
<WHAT KIND OF GUY IS THIS PIRO-SAN YOU WORK WITH?>
<QUIET. OTAKU. NICE GUY. LOSER.>

<NO, WHAT I MEAN IS... DO YOU THINK HE'S THE KIND OF GAIJIN THAT WOULD SHACK UP WITH UNDERAGE GIRLS WHILE STAYING IN JAPAN?>

<ERIKA?>

KLATTER

<IT'S OBVIOUS YOUR LITTLE DIET IS DAMAGING YOUR BRAIN.>
<NOW EAT THAT OR I'LL HOLD YOU DOWN AND SPOON IT INTO YOU.>
<YES MA'AM>

FWIP!
DOM.
ED.
NICE WEATHER TODAY.
YEAH.
THESE SHIPS ARE TOO SLOW.
CAN'T BE HELPED.
WE'D BE THERE ALREADY IF THE FIRST TWO SHIPS HADN'T SUNK ON US.
THEY DON'T BUILD THESE THINGS LIKE THEY USED TO. ONE STRAY **H.E.A.T.** ROUND AND DOWN THEY GO.
I DON'T REALLY FEEL LIKE SWIMMING TO SHORE AGAIN.
WUSS.

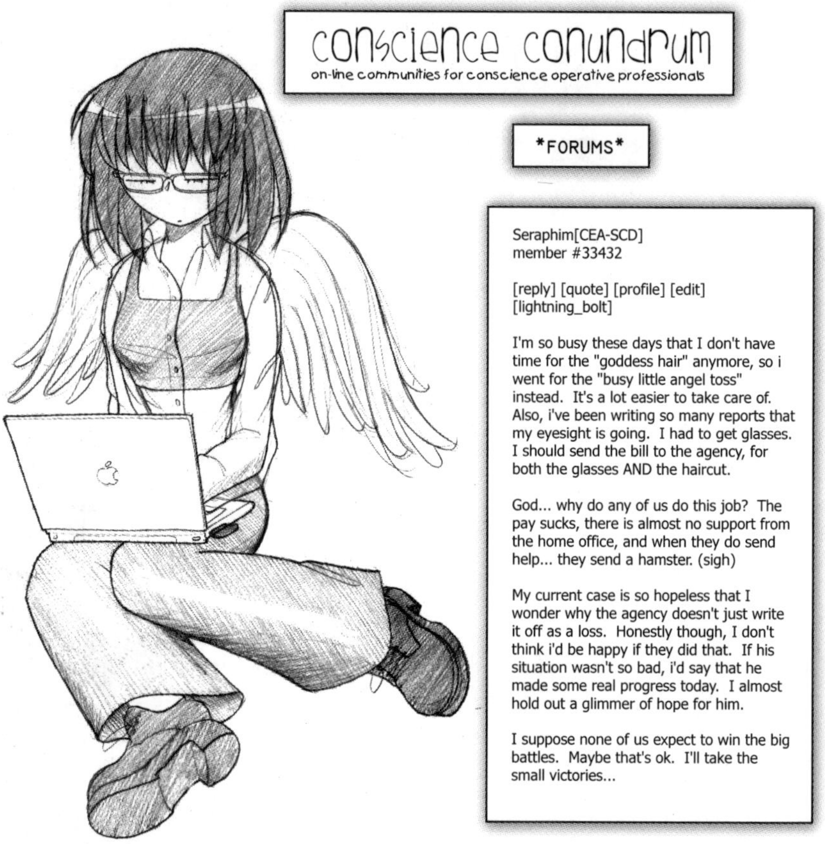

conscience conundrum

on-line communities for conscience operative professionals

FORUMS

Seraphim[CEA-SCD]
member #33432

[reply] [quote] [profile] [edit]
[lightning_bolt]

I'm so busy these days that I don't have time for the "goddess hair" anymore, so i went for the "busy little angel toss" instead. It's a lot easier to take care of. Also, i've been writing so many reports that my eyesight is going. I had to get glasses. I should send the bill to the agency, for both the glasses AND the haircut.

God... why do any of us do this job? The pay sucks, there is almost no support from the home office, and when they do send help... they send a hamster. (sigh)

My current case is so hopeless that I wonder why the agency doesn't just write it off as a loss. Honestly though, I don't think i'd be happy if they did that. If his situation wasn't so bad, i'd say that he made some real progress today. I almost hold out a glimmer of hope for him.

I suppose none of us expect to win the big battles. Maybe that's ok. I'll take the small victories...

...maybe tomorrow's battles won't be so bad.

SO MUCH FOR SOMETHING TO DO ON THE TRIP OVER.
THESE X-BOX CONSOLES ARE ALREADY SO FULL OF PURE EVIL THAT THERE'S NOTHING I CAN ADD.
HOW BORING.
END CHAPTER I

HI EVERYONE! WELCOME ONCE AGAIN TO "LEAVE IT TO SERAPHIM!", WHERE WE TAKE A CLOSER LOOK AT THE HIGH FASHION WORLD OF *MEGATOKYO!*

TODAY, WE'RE GOING TO TAKE A CLOSER LOOK AT EVERY GIRL'S FRIEND, ACCESSORIES!

EVEN WHEN CUTE, ACCESSORIES CAN BE OVERDONE. ERIKA, HON, LIGHTEN UP A LITTLE ON THE HEADGEAR.

HAIR CLIPS ARE GREAT ACCESSORIES! CHEER UP, DEAR, YOU LOOK ADORABLE!

NOW GUYS, PLEASE BE MORE CAREFUL WITH ACCESSORIES. A BEADED NECKLACE AND NO SHIRT? HELP! CALL THE FASHION POLICE!!

BECAUSE THE CAMERA WORK IN MEGATOKYO IS SO TERRIBLE, WE SOMETIMES DON'T EVEN GET TO SEE THE CUTEST ACCESSORIES.

LET'S TAKE A LOOK, SHALL WE? **SERAPHIM CHECK!!**

HERE WE CAN SEE KIMIKO WEARING SOME **VERY** CUTE CLIPS IN HER HAIR, BUT HERE'S WHAT YOU CAN'T SEE...

check point!!
AREN'T THESE SOCKS JUST CUTE AS CAN BE? ENOUGH TO SET OFF PIRO'S SECRET LITTLE SOCK FETISH IF YOU ASK ME!

THAT'S IT FOR TODAY! TUNE IN NEXT TIME FOR ANOTHER "LEAVE IT TO SERAPHIM!!"

OH GOD, NOT ANOTHER HAMSTER. SHOO, SHOO, GO AWAY.

OI. LADY.

メガトーキョー
megatokyo®
<"ARE YOU IN LOVE WITH THAT GUY?">
<"WOO, WAS THAT A LOVE DIARY?">
<HMPH. THEY CAN THINK WHATEVER THEY WANT TO. I DON'T CARE.>
<I DON'T EXPECT THEM TO UNDERSTAND. THEY ARE TOO IMMATURE.>
(SIGH...)
<AFTER SCHOOL, I'M JUST GOING TO ASK HIM. IT CAN'T POSSIBLY BE MORE EMBARRASSING THAN WHAT HAPPENED YESTERDAY.>
<I'LL NEVER FORGIVE MYSELF IF I DON'T.>
chapter 2:
"things change little by little..."

<FEELING BETTER TODAY, YUKI?>
<YES PAPA, MUCH BETTER.>
<GOOD THING. DAD WAS READY TO CALL THE LARGE ANIMAL VET.>
<MOO.>
URK!!
STOMP!
<WHAT WAS THAT FOR?>
<DORK.>
<WOOOO.>
<WELL, YUKI SURE SEEMS TO HAVE RECOVERED QUICKLY.>
<WHAT WAS IT? SOME SORT OF HEAD COLD?>
<THE WORST KIND. WHEN I WAS HER AGE, IT TOOK ME DAYS TO RECOVER FROM BEING LOVESICK.>
<JERK!>
<OHH, WHAT AN UGLY FACE!>
<LOVESICK?>
<MAMA, MAKE YUUJI LEAVE ME ALONE.>
<YUUJI, BE NICE.>
<I DIDN'T DO ANY-THING.>
<MEIMI-SAN? WHAT WAS... YOU SAID, DID YOU SAY-->
BREEEEEP! BREEEEEP!
EEEEEP! BREEEEEP!
<LET ME GET THIS.>
<HELLO, INSPECTOR SONODA, TOKYO POLICE CATACLYSM DIVISION.>
<WHAT? A 300 METER TALL GIANT TURTLE WREAKING HAVOC IN TOKYO BAY?>
<I THOUGHT HE WAS IN REHAB! WHAT? HE WAS LET OUT ON GOOD BEHAVIOR?? WHY DOESN'T ANYONE TELL ME THESE THINGS???
<I GUESS THAT MEANS YOU'LL BE LATE AGAIN TONIGHT. I'LL MAKE YOU A BIGGER LUNCH.
<DAMMIT. WE JUST REBUILT THOSE DOCKS LAST WEEK.>
<STUPID TURTLE.>
<BAI BAI! MAMA, PAPA!>

KNOCK
KNOCK
<YES, YES, HANG ON A MINUTE...>
WHO COULD IT BE AT THIS UNGODLY HOUR...
<ERR...>
<GOOD MORNING. IS PING-CHAN READY FOR SCHOOL?>
<WAI!! TOHYA-SAN! GOOD MORNING!!>
<HUH?? SCHOOL? BUT PING... SHE... SHE'S...>
<READY FOR SCHOOL, PING-CHAN?>
<SCHOOL?>
CLOCKED
-beep-
<AAAAGH!!! I'M GONNA BE LATE!! I HAVE TO CHANGE!!!>
<EXCUSE ME!!>
SLAM
ZZZZ... OOF. ZZZ...
THUD
<YOU HAVEN'T CRACKED THE PERSONAL PRIVACY ALGORITHMS YET? THAT'S PRETTY PATHETIC.>
<AT LEAST LARGO FELL ASLEEP WITH HIS PANTS ON LAST NIGHT.>
ZZZ... ZOMZEES... ZZZ

<KYAAAA!! WHERE'S MY SKIRT??>
ZZZ...

ZZZ... DIE FOOLZZZ DIEEE...

<SO MUCH LIKE A REAL GIRL, ISN'T SHE?>

<PING?>
<WELL... ER... YEAH, I GUESS SO.>

<IS SHE MORE REAL TO YOU THAN I AM?>

<HUH?>

ZZZZ... (SNORT) OH YEAH... YEAAAAHHHH...

<I ASSUME THAT IT IS A GOOD THING I'M LOOKING THE OTHER WAY.>
<ER... LET ME COVER HIM WITH THIS PIECE OF SHEET METAL.>

<THERE. MUCH BETTER.>
<HIS FANTASIES ARE QUITE REAL TO HIM, AREN'T THEY?>
<LARGO? ER, YEAH. HE GETS CARRIED AWAY SOME-TIMES.>
<YOU KEEP **YOUR** FANTASIES TO YOURSELF, THOUGH, DON'T YOU?>
<MY... FANTASIES?>
<MAKES YOU A LITTLE LESS THAN HONEST, DOESN'T IT?>
<TOHYA-SAN! I'M READY!!>
<AH. SHALL WE GO THEN? WE ARE ALREADY LATE.>
<SORRY. IT TOOK FOREVER TO GET MY HAIR RIGHT.>
LESS HONEST? THAN LARGO?
YOU'VE GOTTA BE KIDDING.
THIS IS GARBAGE, OR I'M BURIED UNDER DIRTY LAUNDRY AGAIN... THE FUMES.... IT'S GETTING... DARK....
HELP! A GRUE IS MUNCHING ON MY TOES!

<NANASAWA....>

<WHAT KIND OF IMPOSSIBLE LATCHING DEVICE DID YOU SEW IN THIS TIME?>

<I'M SORRY. HERE, LET ME GET IT.>
<WHY DO YOU MAKE THESE DRESSES SO COMPLICATED?>
<WELL, THEY JUST ARE. YOU LOOK ADORABLE IN FRILLS LIKE THESE.>

<BESIDES, I FIGURE IF I MAKE THE DRESS REAL HARD TO GET OUT OF, IT'LL KEEP YOU OUT OF TROUBLE.>
<ACK, THIS BOW IS ALL WRONG...>

<REMIND ME AGAIN... WHO HAS AN AUDITION FOR A VOICE PART IN A PORN GAME TODAY?>
<EHHHHH... >

leftbehindinemptyplace

<ERIKA, I HAVE TO GO. I NEED TO BE THERE BY NINE.>
<NANASAWA...>
<YOU'RE MORE TALENTED THAN YOU GIVE YOURSELF CREDIT.>
<YOU PUT MORE HEART INTO IT THAN ANY OF THEM DESERVE.>
<GOOD LUCK.>
<THANK YOU... I'LL DO MY BEST.>
KEIO 高井戸駅
<WHERE'S MY RAIL CARD?>
<I KNOW ITS IN HERE...>
<OH.>
<I NEVER DID USE IT AGAIN AFTER THAT DAY.>
BAKA.

LARGO, WHAT ARE YOU DOING?
I AM TAKING INVENTORY OF OUR RE-SOURCES.
L33T M3
IT DOES NOT LOOK GOOD.
PS2. TOSHIBA LAPTOP. VARIOUS TIGER GAMES. HELLO KITTY WRISTWATCH.
WE ARE NOT L33T.
ASK ME IF I CARE.
I'M TIRED AND I WANT TO GO HOME.
IT'D BE NICE IF YOU TRIED TO GET A JOB OR SOMETHING.
DEATH BY ANIME NEW YORK
CHILL, DUDE. I'M SURE WE'LL GET DEPORTED EVENTUALLY.
REMEMBER THAT ROADTRIP WE TOOK TO CANADA?
L33T M3
ACTUALLY, I WAS KIND OF HOPING TO AVOID THAT EXPERIENCE AGAIN.
HEY COME ON! WE GOT HANDCUFFED BY REAL MOUNTIES! THAT WAS COOL.
L33T M3

OK, I NEED TO GO TO WORK.

DON'T MESS WITH MY LAP-TOP OR THAT PS2, OK?

TRUST ME.

L33T M3

JUST... DON'T BREAK OR BLOW UP ANYTHING.

MEGAGAMERS

HMMM...
I DON'T HAVE THE TOOLS TO PROPERLY MODIFY THE EQUIPMENT WE HAVE.
THAT AND I AM ALSO OUT OF DUCT TAPE.
I MUST GO IN SEARCH OF MORE L33T HARD-WARE
YO, DUDE, I'M GONNA DO SOME DUMPSTER DIVING.
DUMPSTER DIVING?
YES. COMPANIES ARE ALWAYS THROWING AWAY PERFECTLY GOOD EQUIPMENT. DIGGING THROUGH THEIR TRASH CAN BE VERY PROFITABLE.
<OI, PIRO, I'LL BE BACK IN A LITTLE WHILE...>
<SO, THIS IS YOUR ROOMATE?>
WOAH.
BAB3-O-R4M4.
ARE THOSE REAL?
<OK, LARGO, HAVE FUN DIGGIN THRU THE GARBAGE!>
FLY YOU FOOL, YOU KNOW NOT YOUR PERIL!
WHA... WHAT'D I DO?

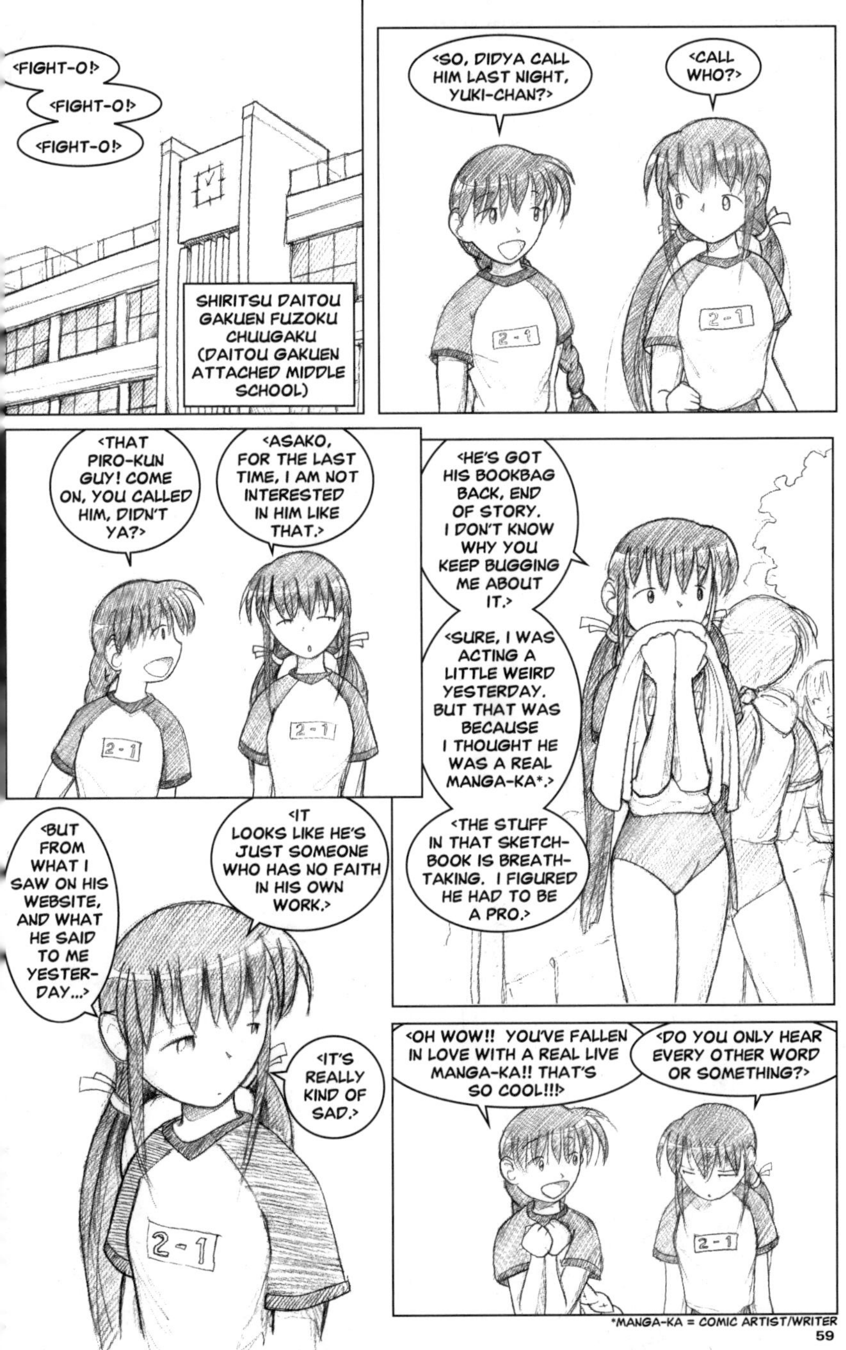

<FIGHT-O!>
<FIGHT-O!>
<FIGHT-O!>
SHIRITSU DAITOU GAKUEN FUZOKU CHUUGAKU (DAITOU GAKUEN ATTACHED MIDDLE SCHOOL)
<SO, DIDYA CALL HIM LAST NIGHT, YUKI-CHAN?>
<CALL WHO?>
2-1
2-1
<THAT PIRO-KUN GUY! COME ON, YOU CALLED HIM, DIDN'T YA?>
<ASAKO, FOR THE LAST TIME, I AM NOT INTERESTED IN HIM LIKE THAT.>
2-1
2-1
<HE'S GOT HIS BOOKBAG BACK, END OF STORY. I DON'T KNOW WHY YOU KEEP BUGGING ME ABOUT IT.>
<SURE, I WAS ACTING A LITTLE WEIRD YESTERDAY. BUT THAT WAS BECAUSE I THOUGHT HE WAS A REAL MANGA-KA*.>
<THE STUFF IN THAT SKETCH-BOOK IS BREATH-TAKING. I FIGURED HE HAD TO BE A PRO.>
<BUT FROM WHAT I SAW ON HIS WEBSITE, AND WHAT HE SAID TO ME YESTER-DAY...>
<IT LOOKS LIKE HE'S JUST SOMEONE WHO HAS NO FAITH IN HIS OWN WORK.>
<IT'S REALLY KIND OF SAD.>
2-1
<OH WOW!! YOU'VE FALLEN IN LOVE WITH A REAL LIVE MANGA-KA!! THAT'S SO COOL!!!>
<DO YOU ONLY HEAR EVERY OTHER WORD OR SOMETHING?>
2-1

*MANGA-KA = COMIC ARTIST/WRITER

OK! LET'S GET STARTED WITH TODAY'S ENGLISH LESSON, EH? TODAY WE ARE GOING TO LEARN SOME "CANADIAN" ENGLISH.
Mr. Grier
"Canadian English is Better English"
ITS FUN! MANY AMERICANS EVEN PRETEND TO BE CANADIANS WHEN TRAVELING ABROAD, BECAUSE CANADIANS ARE SO COOL.
LETS START WITH SOME CANADIAN EXPRESSIONS POPULAR RIGHT NOW, EH?
REPEAT AFTER ME:
"NEVERWINTER NIGHTS WILL BE RELEASED WHEN IT IS COMPLETE."
"NEVERWINTER NIGHTS WILL BE RELEASED THIS WINTER."
"IN CANADA IT'S ALWAYS WINTER."
"NEVERWINTER NIGHTS WILL BE RELEASED SOON, WE PROMISE!"
HEY, WAIT... CUT THAT OUT... NO, NOT THE FACE! THAT'S NOT NICE!!
WE WANT GREAT TEACHER LARGO!!
WE WANT GREAT TEACHER LARGO!!
SEE? IF YOU ALL LOVED CANADIAN POP CULTURE RATHER THAN AMERICAN POP CULTURE...
<SIR, THE STUDENTS ARE RIOTING IN THE COURT-YARD, AND THEY ARE WRITING "GREAT TEACHER LARGO" WITH THE LUNCH-ROOM TABLES.>
<GET ME THIS "GREAT TEACHER LARGO"...>

WHAT THIS ON FLOOR?

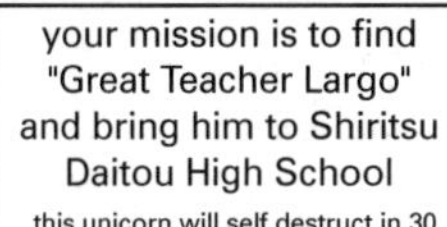
your mission is to find "Great Teacher Largo" and bring him to Shiritsu Daitou High School
this unicorn will self destruct in 30 seconds. for official ninja use only.

IT IS MESSAGE FROM HEAD NINJA.

JUNPEI WONDER...
...IF "GREAT TEACHER LARGO" BE SAME PERSON AS...

THE L33T MASTER...
WOOT! A ROUTER!
WHAT... WHAT THIS? WHY L33T MASTER DIG THRU GARBAGE?
DOES PURSUIT OF L33T LEAVE MASTER POOR AND HUNGRY, LIKE MONK ON GREAT QUEST?
OH, L33T ONE!

WHY? WHY MUST ENLIGHTENED ONES ALWAYS SUFFER?
IS THERE NO JUSTICE?
IS THERE NO HONOR?
JUNPEI! DUDE!
HELP ME DIG OUT THESE SCSI CARDS!
L33T MASTER MUST NOT EAT "SCUZZY" THINGS FROM TRASH.
NOT HEALTHY. GIVE BAD GAS.

<OK, NANASAWA-SAN, WHENEVER YOU ARE READY.>
HAI.
<IN THIS SCENE, THE PROTAGONIST HAS JUST BUMPED INTO KOTONE FOR THE FIRST TIME.>
<SHE SEEMS TO BE A CHEERFUL, GENKI GIRL, FULL OF ENERGY AND LIFE.>
<GENKI AND FULL OF LIFE...>
SIGHT
<I THINK SHE LOOKS... SAD.>
KOTONE
<AND HER STORY...>
<"OH, I'M SORRY. PARDON ME.">
<"EH? ER... NO, I DON'T BELIEVE WE'VE MET BEFORE.">
<"I DON'T THINK... THAT WE COULD HAVE.">
REEHH??
<"WHAT I MEAN IS, I'M NOT EXACTLY... MEMORABLE.">
<DAMNIT, SHE'S READING IT ALL WRONG.>
<NANA...>
<MATSUI, WAIT.>
<LET HER FINISH.>
<I WANT TO HEAR HER VERSION OF KOTONE.>

HAI = <YES> GENKI = <HEALTHY, ENERGETIC>

<UHM, HAYASAKA-SAN?>
<YES?>
<I WANTED TO THANK YOU FOR SENDING DINNER OVER LAST NIGHT. LARGO AND I APPRECIATED IT.>
<WHAT ARE YOU TALKING ABOUT?>
<EH? ER... NANASAWA-SAN CAME OVER LAST NIGHT WITH TWO SPAGHETTI DINNERS. SHE SAID YOU SENT HER.>
<REALLY.>
<WELL, THAT CLARIFIES A FEW THINGS.>
<NANASAWA WAS SAYING SOMETHING LAST NIGHT ABOUT YOU SHACKING UP WITH SOME JUNIOR HIGH SCHOOL GIRL.>
<LET ME GUESS, IT WAS THAT ONE THAT WAS IN HERE YESTERDAY.>
<WH... WHU... HUH??>
<DID YOU MANAGE TO GET HER TO BRING HER FRIENDS?>

<THANK YOU FOR SHARING YOUR LUNCH WITH ME, TOHYA-SAN.>
<I'M ACTUALLY RATHER SURPRISED THAT YOU CAN EAT NORMAL FOODS.>
<WELL, OF COURSE! AN IMPORTANT PART OF ANY DATE USUALLY INVOLVES FOOD. IT WOULD BE AWKWARD IF I COULDN'T EAT.>
<CAN YOU ABSORB ANY ENERGY FROM THESE FOODS?>
<WELL, SORT OF. SUGARS ARE GOOD, I GET A LOT OF ENERGY FROM SUGARS.>
<AGHHH!>
<I ATE THE WHOLE THING! I'M SO SORRY, TOHYA-SAN!>
<I WASN'T PAYING ATTENTION! I'M SORRY!>
<IT'S OK.>
SNAP
<I'LL GO FIND...>
<SOMETHING ELSE TO EAT.>
NO, JUNPEI, NO! THIS PLACE IS EVIL!! WE NEED WEAPONS! CROSSBOWS! ROCKET LAUNCHERS! RENT-A-ZILLA!
SO MANY STUDENT SAY, L33T MASTER.
BUT YOU HAVE BEEN SUMMONED. WE MUST GO, MINUS WEAPON OR LIZARD.

<OK, LET'S TAKE A SHORT BREAK. NANASAWA-SAN, THERE'S A KITCHEN AROUND THE CORNER IF YOU WANT JUICE OR A FRESH WATER.>
<THANK YOU, I'M FINE.>

<IT LOOKS LIKE THEY'RE ARGUING ABOUT SOME-THING.>

<I'M REALLY SCREWING THIS UP, I CAN TELL.>
(SIGH...)

<ITS ODD. I DON'T REALLY WANT THIS PART. BUT, FOR SOME REASON...>

KOTONE
<I REALLY LIKE THIS CHARACTER. I DON'T KNOW WHY.>

<A GIRL OF NOTHING BUT GRAYS...>

<HIGH SCHOOL... GIRL? ME? WITH... ME? HOW... WHY DOES NANASAWA-SAN THINK THAT I, THAT I...?>
<AAAHHH!! PING-CHAN! SHE THOUGHT PING-CHAN WAS A... WAS A...>
<NONONONO, NANASAWA-SAN GOT IT ALL WRONG! PING-CHAN ISN'T A REAL GIRL, SHE'S JUST A PS2 ACCESSORY!!>
<YOU KNOW! THE "EMOTIONAL DOLL SYSTEM" STUFF THAT SONY IS WORKING ON? PING-CHAN IS A PROTOTYPE!! SHE'S NOT A REAL HIGH SCHOOL GIRL! SHE'S JUST A GAME ACCESSORY!!>
<I'M GOING OUT.>
<WATCH THE STORE.>
<SHE DOESN'T EVEN BELONG TO ME, I'M JUST WATCHING HER FOR A FRIEND!>
<HERE, WAIT! I KNOW THAT THERE'S AN ARTICLE IN ONE OF THESE MAGAZINES!>
VOICE
AH, PIRO...
"I'M NOT SLEEPING WITH A JR. HIGH SCHOOL GIRL, I JUST HAVE A LIFE SIZED DOLL THAT LOOKS LIKE ONE!"
SOUNDS SO MUCH LESS PATHETIC.
I'D QUIT WHILE YOU'RE AHEAD, HON.

I DON'T UNDERSTAND WHY YOU ARE DRAGGING ME HERE. I HAVE BETTER THINGS TO BE DOING.
L33T M3

I AM MOST SORRY, L33T MASTER, YOUR PRESENCE IS REQUIRED. NINJA HEAD OFFICE SAY SO.
YEAH, WELL IT SUCKS. I DON'T...
WOAH!
L33T SENSES TINGLING...

L33T ONE, WE MUST HURRY. HAVE APPOINTMENT...
L33T M3
CAREFUL, JUNPEI! DON'T LOOK INTO HER EYES, SHE'LL TURN YOU INTO A FLESH EATING ZOMBIE!!

WELL, WELL, IF IT ISN'T "GREAT TEACHER LARGO."

LET ME GUESS, A "NINJA DOLL SYSTEM" PS2 ACCESSORY.
NICE HAIR. DID YOU STYLE IT YOURSELF OR DID IT COME LIKE THAT?
STICKS! SHARP, POINTY STICKS! **WHY CAN I NEVER FIND ANY!!**
JUNPEI NEED NEW DAY JOB.

IF YOU ARE BACK TO FINISH YOUR EDUCATION, THE ELEMENTARY SCHOOL IS NEXT DOOR.

DO NOT MOCK ME, YOU CURSE OF THE VOID.

I KNOW WHO YOU ARE NOW.

I KNOW YOUR WEAKNESSES

I WILL NOT REST UNTIL YOU ARE ONCE AGAIN DISPATCHED TO THE DARKNESS.

(SIGH...)

<I DON'T FEEL LIKE PLAYING RIGHT NOW.>

<GO TEACH YOUR CLASS, LARGO-SENSEI.>

leedingonmyfallenpast

IT'S LIKE I'VE TOLD YOU BEFORE, PIRO. A LOT OF PEOPLE JUST AREN'T GOING TO UNDERSTAND YOUR LITTLE HOBBY.
NO MATTER HOW HARD YOU TRY TO EXPLAIN THINGS, PEOPLE WILL USUALLY ASSUME THE WORST.
IT'S HUMAN NATURE. THAT'S WHY YOU REALLY SHOULD WORRY A LITTLE MORE ABOUT APPEARANCES THAN YOU DO.
WHY ME? I DIDN'T DO ANYTHING WRONG.
NOW THEY BOTH THINK I'M EITHER A PERVERT OR A FREAK.
I WANNA GO HOME...
-BONK-
THERE, THERE, WE BOTH KNOW YOU AREN'T EITHER OF THOSE THINGS.
JUST KEEP WORKING TOWARDS YOUR GOAL OF EARNING ENOUGH TO GET HOME, AND I'M SURE THINGS WILL BE FINE.
HEYYY, CHECK THIS OUT!
PAT PAT
-BONK-
BRAND NEW SPECIAL LIMITED EDITION KANON PREMIUM TRADING CARDS! WOO!
Kanon
OH GOOD GOD, NOT YOU. GET ME A BUCKET.
HEYYY BABE!
WELL WELL, THEY GOT YOU WORKIN' A FANBOY OTAKU CASE? WHO'D YOU PISS OFF AT THE MAIN OFFICE?
WOW! I HAVEN'T SEEN THESE BEFORE! I WONDER HOW MUCH THE SET WOULD COST...

BTWJ3RZ
SHE MUST PH34R MY NINJA...

JUST LIKE A GREAT BIG TEDDY BEAR.

BTWJ3RZ

SUCH... POWERFUL FINISHING MOVE...
GOOD THING YOU ARE SO TALL DUDE. SHE COULDN'T REACH YOUR BRAINS.

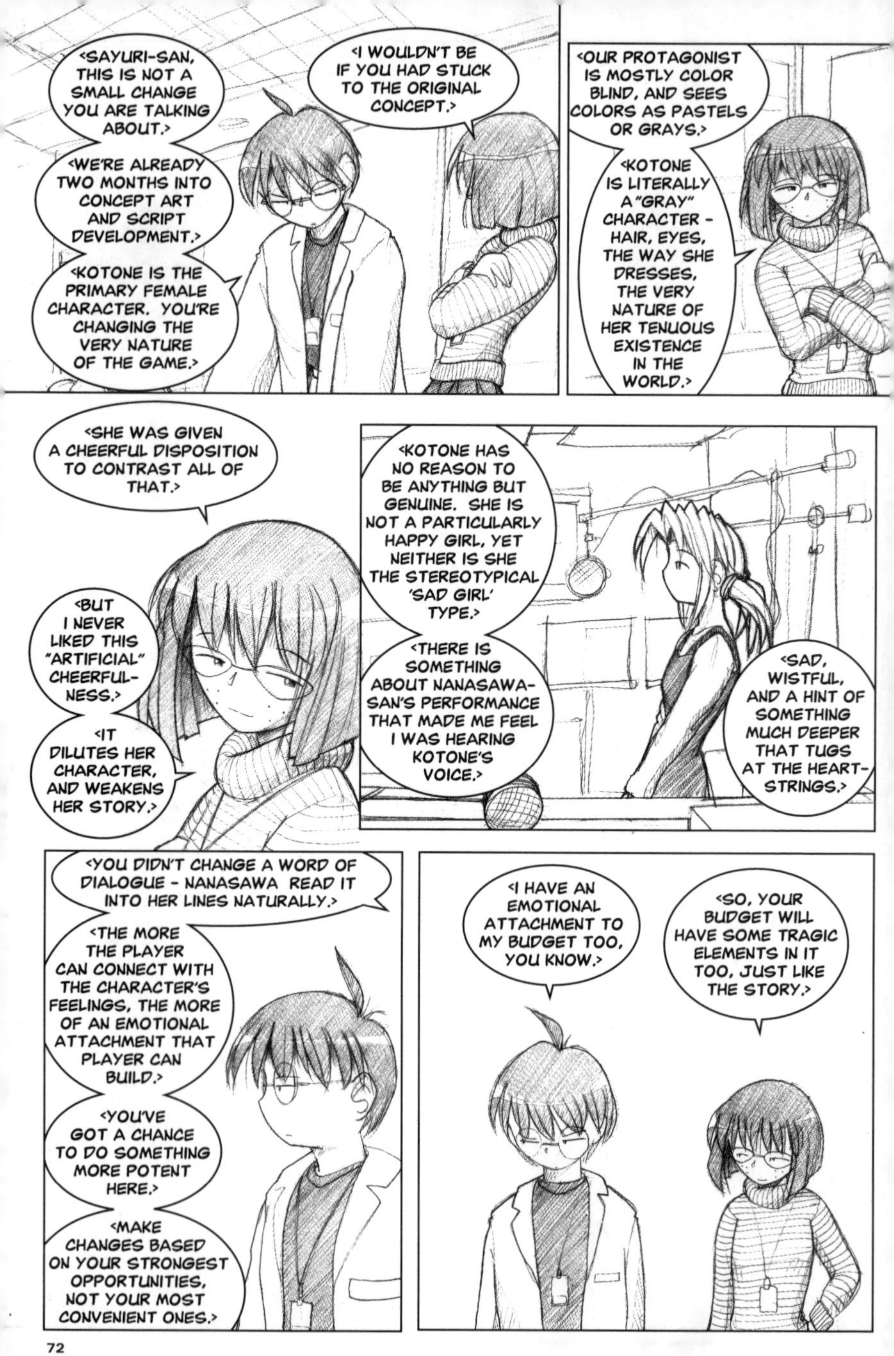

<SAYURI-SAN, THIS IS NOT A SMALL CHANGE YOU ARE TALKING ABOUT.>

<I WOULDN'T BE IF YOU HAD STUCK TO THE ORIGINAL CONCEPT.>

<WE'RE ALREADY TWO MONTHS INTO CONCEPT ART AND SCRIPT DEVELOPMENT.>

<KOTONE IS THE PRIMARY FEMALE CHARACTER. YOU'RE CHANGING THE VERY NATURE OF THE GAME.>

<OUR PROTAGONIST IS MOSTLY COLOR BLIND, AND SEES COLORS AS PASTELS OR GRAYS.>

<KOTONE IS LITERALLY A "GRAY" CHARACTER - HAIR, EYES, THE WAY SHE DRESSES, THE VERY NATURE OF HER TENUOUS EXISTENCE IN THE WORLD.>

<SHE WAS GIVEN A CHEERFUL DISPOSITION TO CONTRAST ALL OF THAT.>
<BUT I NEVER LIKED THIS "ARTIFICIAL" CHEERFUL-NESS.>
<IT DILUTES HER CHARACTER, AND WEAKENS HER STORY.>
<KOTONE HAS NO REASON TO BE ANYTHING BUT GENUINE. SHE IS NOT A PARTICULARLY HAPPY GIRL, YET NEITHER IS SHE THE STEREOTYPICAL 'SAD GIRL' TYPE.>
<THERE IS SOMETHING ABOUT NANASAWA-SAN'S PERFORMANCE THAT MADE ME FEEL I WAS HEARING KOTONE'S VOICE.>
<SAD, WISTFUL, AND A HINT OF SOMETHING MUCH DEEPER THAT TUGS AT THE HEART-STRINGS.>

<YOU DIDN'T CHANGE A WORD OF DIALOGUE - NANASAWA READ IT INTO HER LINES NATURALLY.>

<THE MORE THE PLAYER CAN CONNECT WITH THE CHARACTER'S FEELINGS, THE MORE OF AN EMOTIONAL ATTACHMENT THAT PLAYER CAN BUILD.>

<YOU'VE GOT A CHANCE TO DO SOMETHING MORE POTENT HERE.>

<MAKE CHANGES BASED ON YOUR STRONGEST OPPORTUNITIES, NOT YOUR MOST CONVENIENT ONES.>

<I HAVE AN EMOTIONAL ATTACHMENT TO MY BUDGET TOO, YOU KNOW.>

<SO, YOUR BUDGET WILL HAVE SOME TRAGIC ELEMENTS IN IT TOO, JUST LIKE THE STORY.>

<YUKI-CHAN, WANNA GO SHOPPING AFTER SCHOOL?>

<EH? UHM, ER, I'VE GOT SOME THINGS I HAVE TO DO THIS AFTERNOON.>
<MAYBE WE CAN GO TOMORROW?>

<SOUNDS KIND OF SUSPICIOUS, DOESN'T IT?.>
<YOU THINK SHE'S GONNA GO SEE THAT GUY AGAIN? SHE WAS TALKING ABOUT HIM IN GYM CLASS.>
<I WOULDN'T BE SURPRISED.>
<HEY, STOP TALKING LIKE I'M NOT HERE.>

<WILL YOU PLEASE STOP TEASING ME ABOUT WHAT HAPPENED YESTERDAY?>
<I'M NEVER GOING TO SEE HIM AGAIN. I NEVER HAD ANY FEELINGS FOR HIM AT ALL.>
<LEAVE IT ALONE.>

<COME ON, YUKI, WE'RE YOUR FRIENDS. IT'S SO RARE FOR YOU TO SHOW EVEN SLIGHT INTEREST IN A GUY THAT WE CAN'T JUST LET YOU DROP IT.>
<WE ONLY TEASE YOU BECAUSE WE'RE HAPPY FOR YOU AND WE SUPPORT YOU.>

<AND THAT'S WHY WE'RE COMING WITH YOU TO MAKE SURE YOU DON'T CHICKEN OUT AGAIN.>
<AH, SO YOU ARE GOING TO SEE HIM. I THOUGHT SO.>
<UWAHEEEEEE??? NO! YOU CANT!!>
<WAI! THIS IS BETTER THAN SHOPPING! DO YOUR BEST, YUKI-CHAN!>

WELL WELL, IF IT ISN'T THE GREAT SERAPHIM HERSELF. THIS GUY MUST BE A REAL LOSER TO HAVE YOU DOING THE FIELD WORK.
ASMODEUS. WHAT ARE YOU DOING IN JAPAN? I THOUGHT YOU WERE RUINING THE LIVES OF DOT-COM'ERS IN THE STATES?
NAH, THAT GOT BORING. IT WAS FUN WHEN THEY ALL HAD MONEY, BUT NOW THAT THEY'RE ALL BROKE THEY JUST GET WEEPY ON ME.
WOW, I'LL NEED TO GET SOME MORE CARD PROTEC-TORS...
PIRO...
ER, SORRY.
YOU'RE WASTING YOUR TIME ON THIS "GOOD CONSCIENCE" SHTICK. MY ORGANIZATION HAS BETTER PAY, BETTER BENEFITS, AND COOLER OPERATIVES. WE GOT STYLE.
C'MON, BABE, WHADDYA SAY? MAYBE YOU AND ME COULD WORK OUT A LITTLE... "SIGNING BONUS" TOO.
PHHHT. IN YOUR DREAMS, BAT BOY.
I ALREADY HAVE A PARTNER, AND HE'S FAR SEXIER THAN YOU ARE.
SQUEEEEK!!
HEY, LITTLE DUDE! JUNPEI AND I ARE GONNA TEACH CONTROLLER TECHNIQUE IN CLASS TODAY!
WANNA GRAB THAT ONE I JUST DROPPED?

POOR CONTROLLER TECHNIQUE WILL NOT BE TOLERATED! IT CAN LEAD TO M4D B34TDOWNZ.
B34DOWNZ SUXOR!
BEETSU-DOWNZU SUKSORU!

THE CONSOLE IS A CONDUIT FOR THE SOUL.
THE CONTROLLER IS YOUR GATEWAY. LIVE THRU IT. FEEL THRU IT. YOU MUST BE ONE WITH YOUR GAME PAD.

THE ONLY WAY TO DESTROY YOUR OPPONENT IS TO POUR YOUR VERY LIFE AND SOUL INTO IT. IF YOU DO NOT, YOU WILL BE ROXOR3D...

BY THE FORCES OF DARKNESS THAT PLAGUE OUR WORLD! PH34R THEM! FOR THEY WALK AMONG...
ER...

WHERE DID THE 3VIL ONE GO?

<SENSEI, TOHYA-SAN SAID THAT SHE WASN'T FEELING WELL. SHE TOLD ME TO STAY HERE AND WOULDN'T LET ME COME WITH HER. I'M VERY WORRIED, SENSEI, I THINK SHE MIGHT BE VERY SICK.>

HOW DARE SHE SKIP MY CLASS!!!!
<ACTUALLY, I SAW TOHYA EARLIER TOO, AND SHE DIDN'T LOOK SO GOOD.>
<I WONDER IF SHE'S SICK AGAIN?>

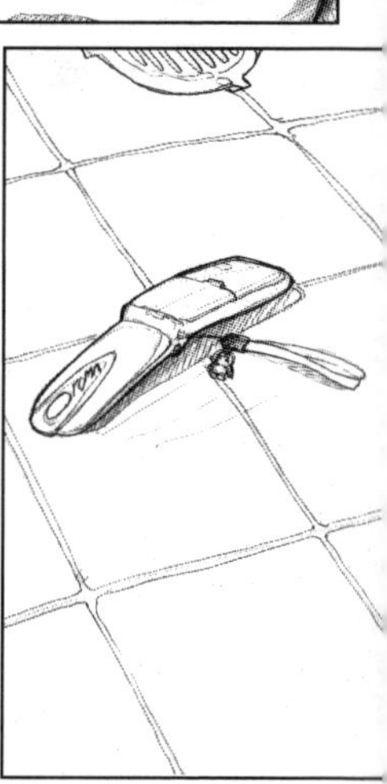

SENSEI! TAIHEN DESU!!
SWISH!
I DON'T FEEL HER PRESENCE. WHY DID SHE ABANDON THE BATTLE?

<A STUDENT HAS COLLAPSED IN THE GIRLS BATHROOM!! I THINK IT'S TOHYA-SAN FROM YOUR CLASS!!>

WHAT IS THIS ONE BABBLING ABOUT?
SHE SAY THERE GIRL STUDENT COLLAPSED IN BATHROOM.

AND SO THE BODY COUNT BEGINS...
I KNEW I SHOULDA BROUGHT A CROSSBOW.
<NO, SENSEI, THIS WAY!>
L33T MASTER!
L33 ME

I WILL GO ALONE.
BACK! YOU MAY NOT SURVIVE THE HORROR!

WH... WHAT MOCKERY IS THIS?

<TOHYA-SAN!!>
<ARE YOU OK?>
<PLEASE WAKE UP!!>
<TOHYA-SAN?>
<TOHYA-SAN...>
<HER PULSE IS WEAK AND THREADY...>
<SHE'S COLD... BARELY BREATHING...>
<SHE NEEDS MEDICAL ATTENTION. I HAVE TO GET HELP!>
LARGO-SENSEI,
ONEGAI DESU....
TOHYA-SAN WO...
TOHYA-SAN WO TASUKETE AGETE KUDASAI....
JUNPEI...
GATHER THE FALLEN.
I WILL NOT ACCEPT...
AN ENDING WITHOUT HONOR.

<NANASAWA-SAN THANK YOU FOR COMING INTO THE STUDIO TODAY. WE APPRECIATE YOUR EFFORTS.>

<AS YOU'VE READ, "SIGHT" IS A RATHER DEEP AND EMOTIONAL VISUAL NOVEL. KIND OF THE TREND THESE DAYS.>
<KOTONE IS AN IMPORTANT CHARACTER IN THE GAME, AND ALL THE SCENARIOS REVOLVE AROUND HER IN SOME WAY.>

<WE WERE BOTH PARTICULARLY IMPRESSED WITH YOUR PERFORMANCE, BUT...>
<I HAVE RESERVATIONS ABOUT CHANGING THE NATURE OF KOTONE'S CHARACTER THIS LATE IN THE PROCESS.>
<CHANGING?>

<YOUR READING OF KOTONE GIVES HER A DIFFERENT PERSONALITY THAN SHE CURRENTLY HAS. IF WE GIVE YOU THE PART, WE HAVE TO CHANGE THE STORY.>
<OBVIOUSLY, THAT'S NOT A DECISION TO BE MADE LIGHTLY.>

<WE SHOULD BE ABLE TO LET YOU KNOW BY THE END OF DAY TOMOR-ROW.>

BIGE
<"IF WE GIVE YOU THE PART, WE HAVE TO CHANGE THE STORY.">

(SIGH...)
<I GUESS THEY DON'T REALIZE I'M USED TO REJECTION.>
<IF ONLY THEY KNEW HOW USED TO IT I AM...>

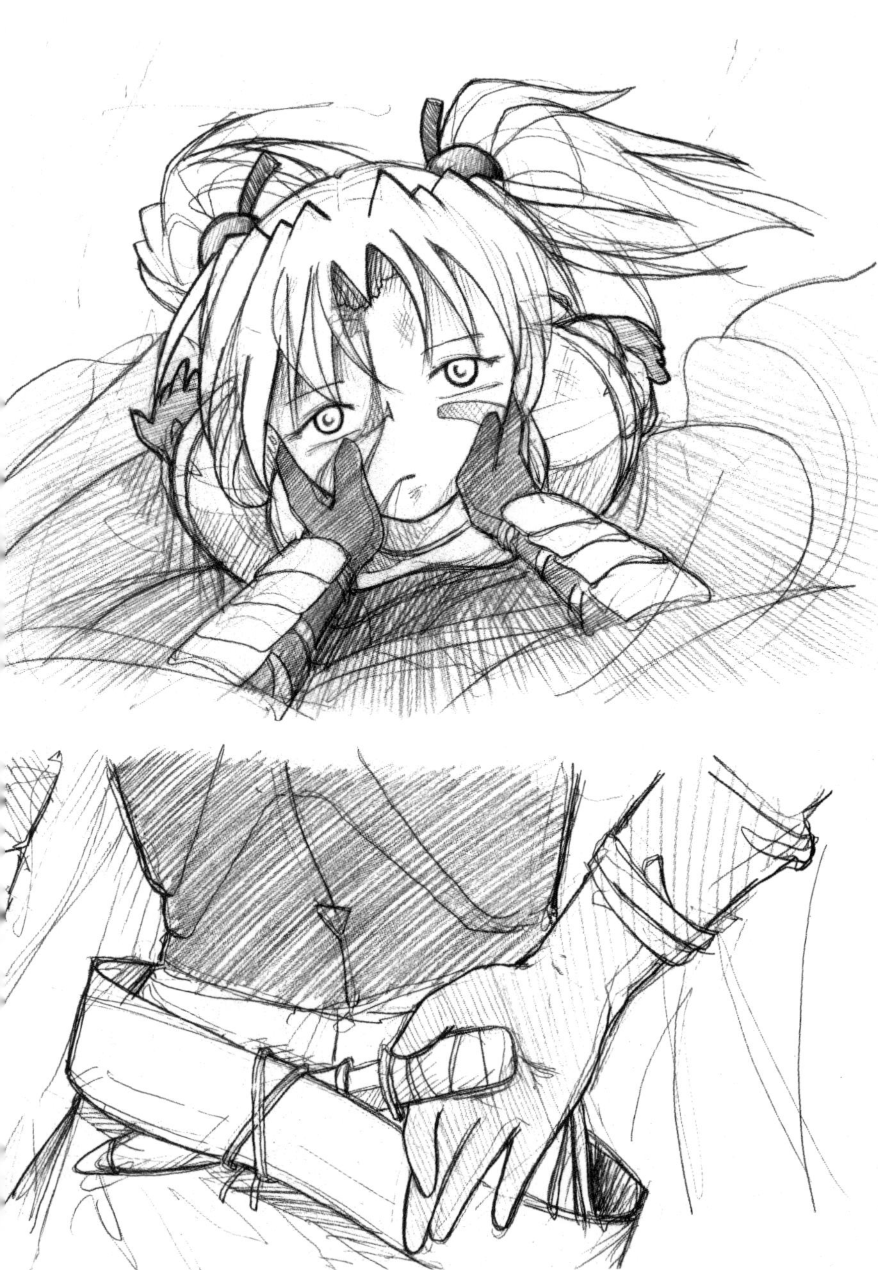

L33T MASTER.
JUNPEI TAKE GIRL TO NURSE OFFICE.
DO WHAT YOU MUST.
WHAT IS THIS?
IT APPEARS TO BE SOME SORT OF INTER-DIMENSIONAL COMMUNI-CATIONS DEVICE.
I CANNOT READ THESE EVIL RUNES.
WAS SHE ATTEMPTING TO CALL FORTH EVIL MINIONS?
IS THIS DEVICE USED TO RAISE UNDEAD ARMIES?
FOMA
THERE IS SOMETHING ELSE... SOME-THING ABOUT THIS PLACE...
SOMETHING UNUSUAL...
OH YEAH! I'VE NEVER BEEN IN A GIRL'S BATHROOM BEFORE! COOL!
<SENSEI. GET OUT.>
<NOW.>
L33T M3

-BRRRRRRRTTTTTTTTTTTTTT!!-
CLANG!

SEGA

KERCHACK-

DOM.
ED.
LOOKS LIKE WE'RE HERE.
NO THANKS TO YOU.

TRAVELING SURE IS A PAIN THESE DAYS.
I REALLY DON'T UNDERSTAND WHY THEY WON'T LET US FLY.

<JUNPEI WILL LEAVE GIRL IN YOUR CARE.>
<THANK YOU FOR BRINGING HER DOWN HERE.>
<TOHYA-SAN HAS HAD THESE FAINTING SPELLS BEFORE.>
<SHE'LL BE FINE, SHE JUST NEEDS SOME REST. I'LL CALL HER PARENTS.>
<TOHYA-SAN? DID I DO SOMETHING WRONG? IS IT MY FAULT YOU ARE SICK? PLEASE WAKE UP.>
<HM, NO ANSWER. I CAN NEVER REACH TOHYA'S PARENTS FOR SOME REASON...>
<I DON'T UNDERSTAND ANY OF THESE READINGS. DO YOU KNOW WHAT'S WRONG WITH TOHYA-SAN?>
<READINGS?>
<UH HUH. VITAL SIGNS. PULSE, BLOOD PRESSURE, TEMPERATURE, ETC.>
<EMOTIONAL DOLL SYSTEM UNITS LIKE MYSELF ARE EQUIPPED WITH BASIC MONITORING EQUIPMENT AND LIMITED MEDICAL KNOWLEDGE.>
<OUR TARGET MARKET TENDS TO TAKE POOR CARE OF THEMSELVES AND CAN HAVE SERIOUS HEALTH PROBLEMS.>
<WE'RE SORT OF LIKE "VIRTUAL PETS," EXCEPT WE CAN TAKE CARE OF OUR END USERS.>
<"VIRTUAL PETS"? SO YOU ARE A... A... OH DEAR.>
<DO YOU HAVE A DATA OUTLET SOMEWHERE? I WANT TO GET ONLINE AND RESEARCH HER SYMPTOMS MORE.>

<LOOK, I JUST WANT TO ASK HIM ABOUT SOMETHING. IT'S NO BIG DEAL.>
<YOU'RE GONNA ASK HIM OUT ON A DATE? THAT'S SO DARING, YUKI-CHAN!>
<NO! I AM NOT ASKING HIM OUT!!>
<WHAT COULD IT BE THEN? I THINK SHE'S HIDING SOMETHING.>
<I THINK SO TOO. WHY CAN'T SHE JUST BE HONEST WITH HER-SELF? IT'D BE SO MUCH EASIER ON US.>
<HEY...>
<SINCE YOU INSIST ON FOLLOWING ME, YOU'LL SEE FOR YOURSELVES ANYWAY.>
<THEN WHY WON'T YOU TELL US?>
<WELL... BECAUSE... BECAUSE I...>
EXCUSE ME.
HAVE YOU SEEN THIS GUY?
ER...
I AM SORRY. I HAVE NOT SEEN THIS GUY.
ARE YOU SURE? WE'RE PRETTY SURE HE'S BEEN SEEN IN THIS AREA.
NO, I AM SORRY, I NOT SEE THAT PERSON BEFORE. GOMEN!
YOU'D THINK WITH LARGO'S FLAIR FOR "INCIDENTS" THAT SOMEBODY WOULD RECOIL IN HORROR FROM HIS PICTURE.
SHE'S HIDING SOMETHING.
I CAN DROP HER FROM HERE.
ED...

I CAN'T BELIEVE IT.
HAYASAKA-SAN MUST THINK I'M SOME KINDA FREAKY PERVERT OR SOMETHING.

SHE COULD HAVE WAITED FOR ME TO EXPLAIN, THOUGH. WHY DO GIRLS INSIST ON JUMPING TO CONCLUSIONS?
IT'S NOT FAIR.

THEY ALWAYS SEEM TO THINK THE WORST THING POSSIB....
ER...

THE LOOK ON THAT GIRL'S FACE WASN'T SADNESS.
IT WAS A LOOK OF PURE DISGUST.

SHE WAS... DISGUSTED. UTTER REVULSION... NOT SADNESS... IN THOSE EYES.
I... I CAN'T DEAL WITH SOMEONE THINKING THAT ABOUT ME. I... JUST CAN'T.

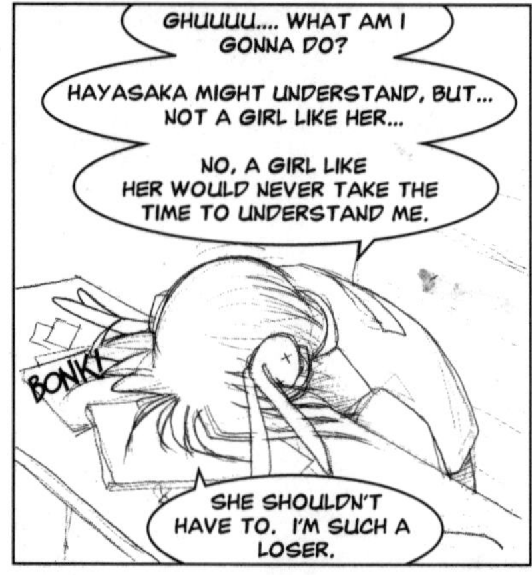
GHUUUU.... WHAT AM I GONNA DO?
HAYASAKA MIGHT UNDERSTAND, BUT... NOT A GIRL LIKE HER...
NO, A GIRL LIKE HER WOULD NEVER TAKE THE TIME TO UNDERSTAND ME.
BONK!
SHE SHOULDN'T HAVE TO. I'M SUCH A LOSER.

IF THIS WERE A GAME, I COULD GO BACK AND LOCK PING IN A CLOSET.
I GUESS I'M HEADING FOR ONE OF THE "BAD" ENDINGS.
MR. PIRO-SAN? CAN... CAN I PLEASE SPEAK WITH YOU?

<I DON'T UNDERSTAND WHY THEY COULDN'T JUST TELL ME THAT I DIDN'T GET THE PART.>

<WHY SUCH AN ELABORATE STORY? WHY NOT JUST "SORRY, YOU AREN'T WHAT WE WE'RE LOOKING FOR.">
<WHY DOES EVERYONE HAVE TO BABY ME?>

<I'M TIRED OF IT. I ALWAYS FEEL LIKE EVERYONE IS JUST BEING NICE AND DON'T WANT TO TELL ME WHAT THEY REALLY THINK.>

<SO WHAT IF I'M NOT CUTE ENOUGH TO LAND A DECENT VOICE ACTING ROLE?>
<SO WHAT IF I GET CRAPPY TIPS BECAUSE I'M NOT "BUILT" LIKE THE OTHER WAITRESSES?>
<SO WHAT IF I WANT TO SUPPORT MYSELF FOR ONCE IN MY LIFE.>
(SIGH...)

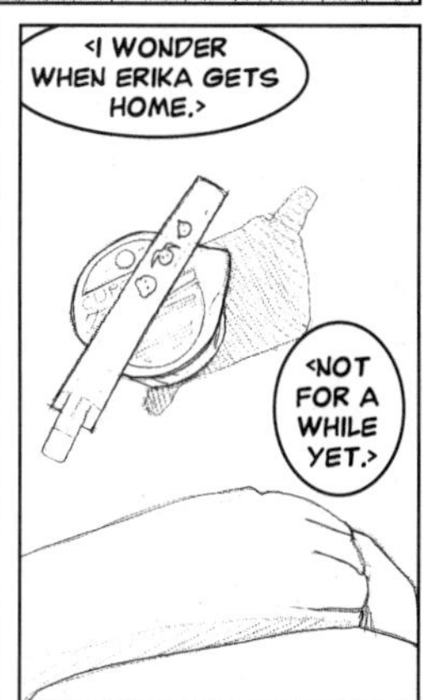
<I WONDER WHEN ERIKA GETS HOME.>
<NOT FOR A WHILE YET.>

<NO, I HAVE TO STOP RUNNING TO ERIKA WHENEVER I HAVE PROBLEMS.>
<I DON'T WANT HER TO ALWAYS HAVE TO FEEL SORRY FOR ME.>

(SNIFF...)

<MAYBE IF I STOPPED FEELING SORRY FOR MYSELF, SHE WOULDN'T HAVE A REASON TO.>
<GOD, I AM SO PATHETIC.>

SPEAK... WITH ME? CAN I... HELP YOU?

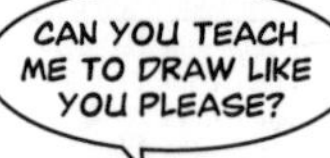
CAN YOU TEACH ME TO DRAW LIKE YOU PLEASE?

HUH?

<WHAT THE HELL KIND OF QUESTION IS THAT?>
<WHAT DID SHE SAY? DID SHE ASK HIM OUT?>

ME?? TEACH?? BUT... I CAN'T DRAW THAT WELL AND THERE ARE FAR BETTER...
I WILL PAY FOR LESSONS.
I WANT TO LEARN HOW YOU DRAW.

BUT... I CAN'T... I MEAN, PEOPLE ALREADY THINK I, THAT I....

THAT I... I MEAN..
EEP....

I CAN PAY FOR LESSONS.
PLEASE TEACH ME TO DRAW.
<WHAT IS YUKI-CHAN DOING?>
<I DON'T HAVE A CLUE.>

CAN I HAVE YOUR ANSWER PLEASE.
WILL YOU TEACH ME TO DRAW?
EH??

I'M SORRY, BUT...
NO, WAIT...
<I'M SORRY, BUT I CAN'T GIVE YOU DRAWING LESSONS. I AM ONLY VISITING JAPAN FOR A SHORT TIME, AND I WILL BE GOING HOME SOON.>
<I'M SORRY, I'M REALLY REALLY SORRY.>

<YOU... CAN'T?...>

<WELL, WELL, IT LOOKS LIKE PIRO'S LITTLE FAN CLUB IS ALL HERE. HOW NICE.>

THIS IS THE LAST PLACE I EXPECTED TO FIND LARGO.
I WONDER WHAT KIND OF SCAM HE'S WORKING THIS TIME.
IT WAS SURPRISING WHEN STUDENTS STARTED TO RECOGNIZE HIM IN THE PICTURE.
I'D STILL LIKE TO KNOW WHAT MADE YOU THINK WE'D FIND HIM AROUND THIS PARTICULAR SCHOOL...
BEEP
SWISH
CLICK
WELL, WELL... THE MISSING EDS PROTOTYPE.
THE BOYS IN THE LAB WERE PRETTY UPSET WHEN YOU WENT MISSING.
OH, AND THANKS FOR PLUGGING INTO THE NETWORK.
MADE MY JOB A LOT EASIER.
<I'M SORRY, I DON'T UNDER-STAND WHAT YOU ARE SAYI-->
SO, YOU COMMIN BACK WHOLE...
OR IN LITTLE PLASTIC PIECES?
EITHER WAY WORKS FOR ME.
<EEP!>
BEEP
MODE: AUTO
THREAT DETECTED
LEVEL 3
<I DON'T KNOW WHAT YOU WANT, BUT I WON'T LET YOU HARM TOHYA-SAN!!>

lthissorrowbecomesme

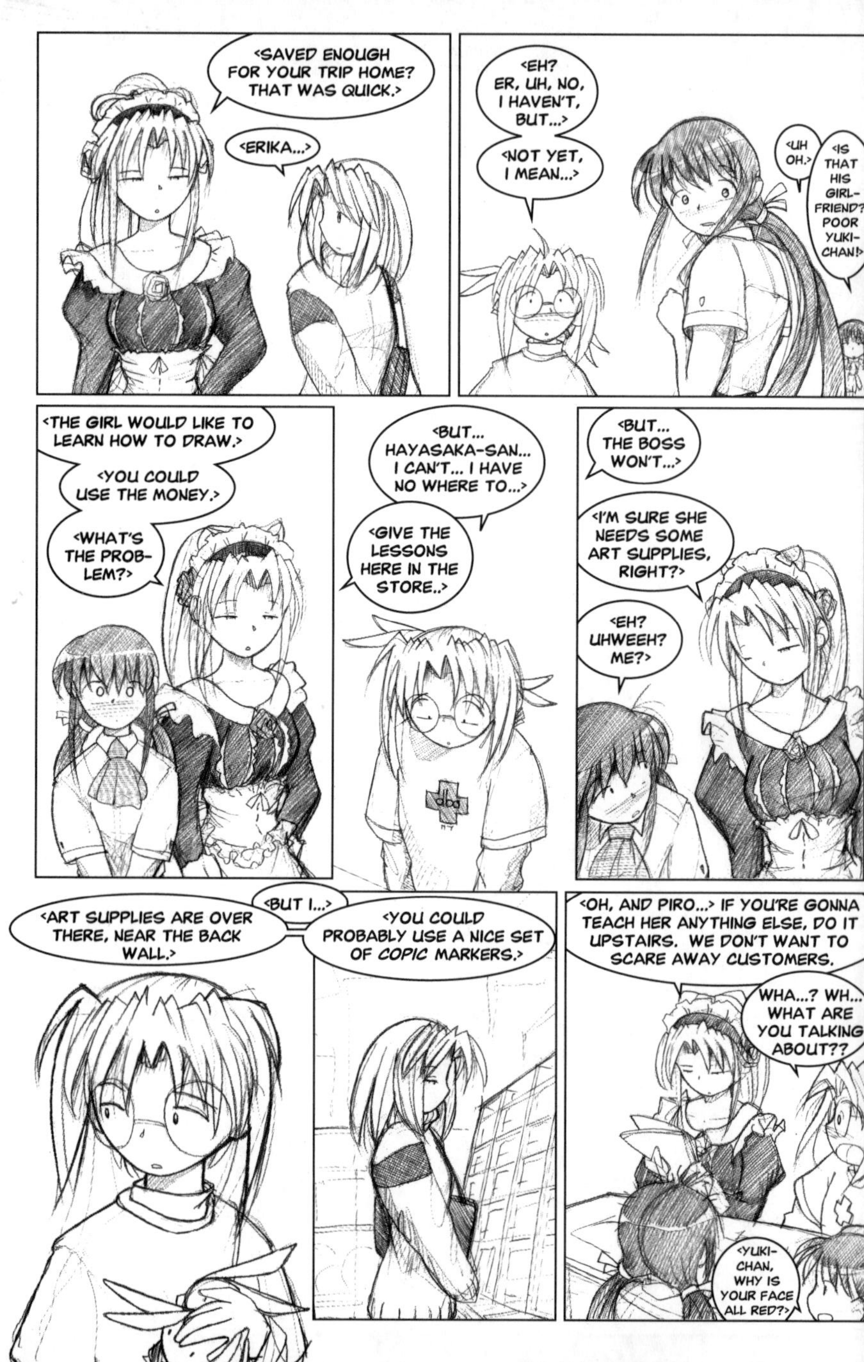
<SAVED ENOUGH FOR YOUR TRIP HOME? THAT WAS QUICK.>
<ERIKA...>
<EH? ER, UH, NO, I HAVEN'T, BUT...>
<NOT YET, I MEAN...>
<UH OH.>
<IS THAT HIS GIRL-FRIEND? POOR YUKI-CHAN!>
<THE GIRL WOULD LIKE TO LEARN HOW TO DRAW.>
<YOU COULD USE THE MONEY.>
<WHAT'S THE PROB-LEM?>
<BUT... HAYASAKA-SAN... I CAN'T... I HAVE NO WHERE TO...>
<GIVE THE LESSONS HERE IN THE STORE..>
<BUT... THE BOSS WON'T...>
<I'M SURE SHE NEEDS SOME ART SUPPLIES, RIGHT?>
<EH? UHWEEH? ME?>
<ART SUPPLIES ARE OVER THERE, NEAR THE BACK WALL.>
<BUT I...>
<YOU COULD PROBABLY USE A NICE SET OF *COPIC* MARKERS.>
<OH, AND PIRO...> IF YOU'RE GONNA TEACH HER ANYTHING ELSE, DO IT UPSTAIRS. WE DON'T WANT TO SCARE AWAY CUSTOMERS.
WHA...? WH... WHAT ARE YOU TALKING ABOUT??
<YUKI-CHAN, WHY IS YOUR FACE ALL RED?>

YOUR HOMEWORK TONIGHT IS TO BREAK OPEN THE CASES ON THOSE L4M3 COMPUTERS YOU HAVE AT HOME AND MAKE THEM L33T USING THE MAD T3CHNIQ3S I'VE SHOWN YOU.
IS THAT CLEAR!!
SWISH
CLACK
YES, GREAT TEACHER LARGO!

DOM!!
1337
M3
HEY LARGO.
DUDE! ZOMBIES AND UNDEAD ARMIES ARE OVERWHELMING TOKYO. YOU BROUGHT LOTSA GUNS WITH YOU, RIGHT?
DON'T I ALWAYS? HOW'S PIRO?

WHUMP!! WHUMPBOOM!!
SQUERK!

WHAT WAS THAT?
EARTH-QUAKE. THEY HAVE A LOT OF THEM HERE IN JAPAN.
SW33T!!!!
EITHER THAT OR ED IS AMUSING HIMSELF BY DETONATING VENDING MACHINES AGAIN.

<MY GOODNESS, WHAT IN THE WORLD WAS THAT NOISE??>
tap tap tap tap tap
<PINGU-SAN, IS EVERYTHING ALL RIGHT? I THOUGHT I HEARD A LOUD...>
<OH, HI, MISS SUGAWARA-SAN.>
<SORRY ABOUT THE MESS. I HAD TO MAKE A BAD MAN GO AWAY.>
<BAD...>
<MAN?>
<UH HUH. IT'S OK, HE'S GONE NOW.>
<I THINK I GOT ALL THE GLASS UP OFF THE FLOOR...>
<WHERE..?>
<OUTSIDE SOMEWHERE.>
<OH, AND I'M SORRY ABOUT THE CONCRETE COLUMN. HIS HEA KINDA CLIPPED IT WHEN I HEAVED HIM OUT THE WINDOW.>

WOW, THIS GUY IS PATHETIC.

WHAT'S HIS PROBLEM? THAT PIG-TAILED CUTIE IS HOT FOR HIM.
SHE'S FIFTEEN. DON'T TALK ABOUT HER THAT WAY.

BAH. WHO CARES? MAYBE I SHOULD GO DOWN AND TALK SOME SENSE INTO HIM.
YOU DO AND YOU'LL BE WALKING FUNNY FOR MONTHS.

Y'KNOW, THIS "MORALITY" CRAP OF YOURS IS NOTHING MORE THAN SEXUAL REPRESSION. NO WONDER HE FANTASIZES OVER LITTLE CARTOON CHICKS.

LET THE GUY HAVE A LITTLE FUN. HE'S IN A FOREIGN COUNTRY. CHICKS HERE DIG FOREIGNERS. WHERE'S THE HARM?
PIRO IS DOING FINE. STAY OUT OF IT.

MAN, TALK ABOUT SOMEONE WHO NEEDS TO LIGHTEN UP. I'D BE MORE THAN HAPPY TO HELP YOU HAVE... A LITTLE FUN... LOOSEN UP A LITTLE.
TOKYO CAN BE A FUN PLACE, WITH THE RIGHT GUIDE...

HMM. LOOKS LIKE THE *APPLE* LOGO IS EMBEDDED IN YOUR FOREHEAD. INTERESTING.
OUCH. CAREFUL WITH THE HAIR, DOC. DON'T TOUCH THE HAIR.

I WONDER...
HOW DOES FAILURE...
TASTE...
FWIIIIP!
I KNOW YOU ARE CHEATING.
AND I KNOW HOW TO BEAT IT.

<AH, YOU'RE AWAKE.>

<I WAS BEGINNING TO WORRY. IT'S GETTING LATE, AND I HAVEN'T BEEN ABLE TO REACH YOUR PARENTS ALL AFTERNOON.>

<YOUR FRIEND HASN'T LEFT YOUR SIDE ALL DAY. SHE'S BEEN VERY WORRIED ABOUT YOU.>

<I NEED YOU TO GIVE ME YOUR PARENTS' CELL PHONE NUMBERS, TOHYA-SAN. ALL THESE FAINTING SPELLS HAVE ME WORRIED.>
<IT'S ONLY BEEN TWO YEARS SINCE YOU WERE IN THE HOSPITAL.>

<HOW...>
<DID I GET HERE?>
<DID YOU BRING ME HERE, PING?>

<I TOLD YOU TO GO AWAY. I TOLD YOU TO NOT FOLLOW ME.>
<I DON'T NEED YOUR PROGRAMMED COMPASSION. I DON'T... NEED YOU.>

<I WANTED TO USE YOU, BUT YOU HAVE NOTHING I NEED. NOTHING. YOU'RE AN EMPTY VESSEL...>
<EMPTY, UNUSED...>

<I CAN'T TAKE ANYTHING FROM YOU. I DON'T NEED YOU... FOR MYSELF...>
<HYWEEEH... TOHYA-SAN?>

<TOHYA-SAN, ARE YOU CRYING? DID I DO SOMETHING WRONG? I'M SORRY! PLEASE, DON'T CRY!>
BAKA... <DON'T LOOK AT ME...>

Death by Anime
NEW YORK
<WELL... IF YOU REALLY WANT TO LEARN HOW TO DRAW...>
I GUESS...
<THANK YOU, MR. PIRO-SENSEI! I WON'T LET YOU DOWN! IS IT OKAY IF I COME HERE TOMORROW AT SEVEN?>
UHM, OK...
<YAY! I'LL SEE YOU TOMORROW THEN!>
<SORRY FOR BOTHERING YOU, SENSEI!>
BAI BAI!
<SO, HOW DID THE AUDITION GO?>
<NOT VERY WELL. I DIDN'T GET THE PART.>
I DON'T SUPPOSE YOU ALSO GIVE VOICE ACTING LESSONS? NANASAWA MIGHT BE INTERESTED.
WILL YOU **PLEASE** STOP TEASING ME?

<LETS START CLOSING UP SHOP, PIRO.>
<OK.>
MEGAGAMERS
メガゲーマーズ

<I BROUGHT YOU A CHANGE OF CLOTHES. I'M SORRY THE DRESS IS SO UNCOMFORTABLE.>
<IT'S NOT THAT BAD. CUSTOMERS SEEMED TO LIKE IT, AS ALWAYS.>

<ACTUALLY, THEY SAID THAT THEY'D HAVE TO REWRITE THE STORY IN ORDER TO GIVE ME THE PART.>
<SO, WHAT HAPPENED?>
<I ASSUME THAT IT DIDN'T GO AS BAD AS YOU THINK IT DID.>
-SWEEP-
-SWEEP-

<IT'S MY FAULT. I'VE BEEN FEELING REALLY DOWN LATELY, AND I DON'T THINK I READ THE LINES RIGHT.>
<HM. THAT'S RATHER COLD.>
<I WASN'T "CHEERFUL" ENOUGH.>
<NANASAWA, IF YOU ARE GOING TO BE A VOICE ACTRESS, YOU'LL HAVE TO LEARN HOW TO BE SICKENINGLY CHEERFUL NO MATTER HOW YOU FEEL.>

<THAT'S WHY THEY CALL IT "ACTING"...>
NANASAWA IS A VOICE ACTRESS?
WOW.

A REAL LIVE VOICE ACTRESS...
AND SHE THINKS I'M LOWER THAN DIRT.

DUDE! DOM AND I JUST SAVED TOKYO FROM THE ZOMBIE HORDES!
(SIGH...)
COULD BE WORSE. LARGO COULD'VE ANSWERED THE DOOR.
IT'S SAPPORO TIME!
-SWEEP-
-SWEEP-

<I'LL GO CHANGE.>
<OK, I'LL BE OUT HERE.>
GYEHHH!! WHAT ARE YOU DOING HERE??
LETS HIT SOME BARS, DUDE!
<DAMN UNDERWEAR IS RIDING UP MY ASS...>
I NEED B33R MOST BADLY.
LARGO. WE'RE BROKE. SOBER UP FOR ONCE IN YOUR LIFE.
BROKE? DUDE, WE AIN'T BROKE...
WE GOT PLENTY OF M4D CA$H.
WHERE DID YOU GET THIS?
DON'T TELL ME YOU BEAT UP SOME KIDS AT AN ARCADE AGAIN...
I AM GREAT TEACHER LARGO!
I AM WELL PAID FOR MY SERVICES!
GREAT... TEACHER... WHAT...?
GREAT TEACHER LARGO!!
I'M TEACHING HIGH SCHOOL KIDS COOL L33T SKILLZ AND STUFF.
FIVE THOUSAND DOLLARS FOR TEACHING JUST TWO CLASSES THIS WEEK!
NOW I KNOW WHY JAPAN HAS SUCH A SUPERIOR EDUCATION SYSTEM. THEY PAY THEIR TEACHERS VERY WELL!
KNOWLEDGE AND L33T SKILLS ARE HONORED AND REVERED HERE!
UH, LARGO. THIS IS FIVE THOUSAND **YEN**. THAT'S LESS THAN FIFTY DOLLARS.
I FEEL THE NEED TO B4TH3 IN B33R.
SO, WHAT ARE YOU TEACHING? STUPIDITY?
SWEEP SWEEP

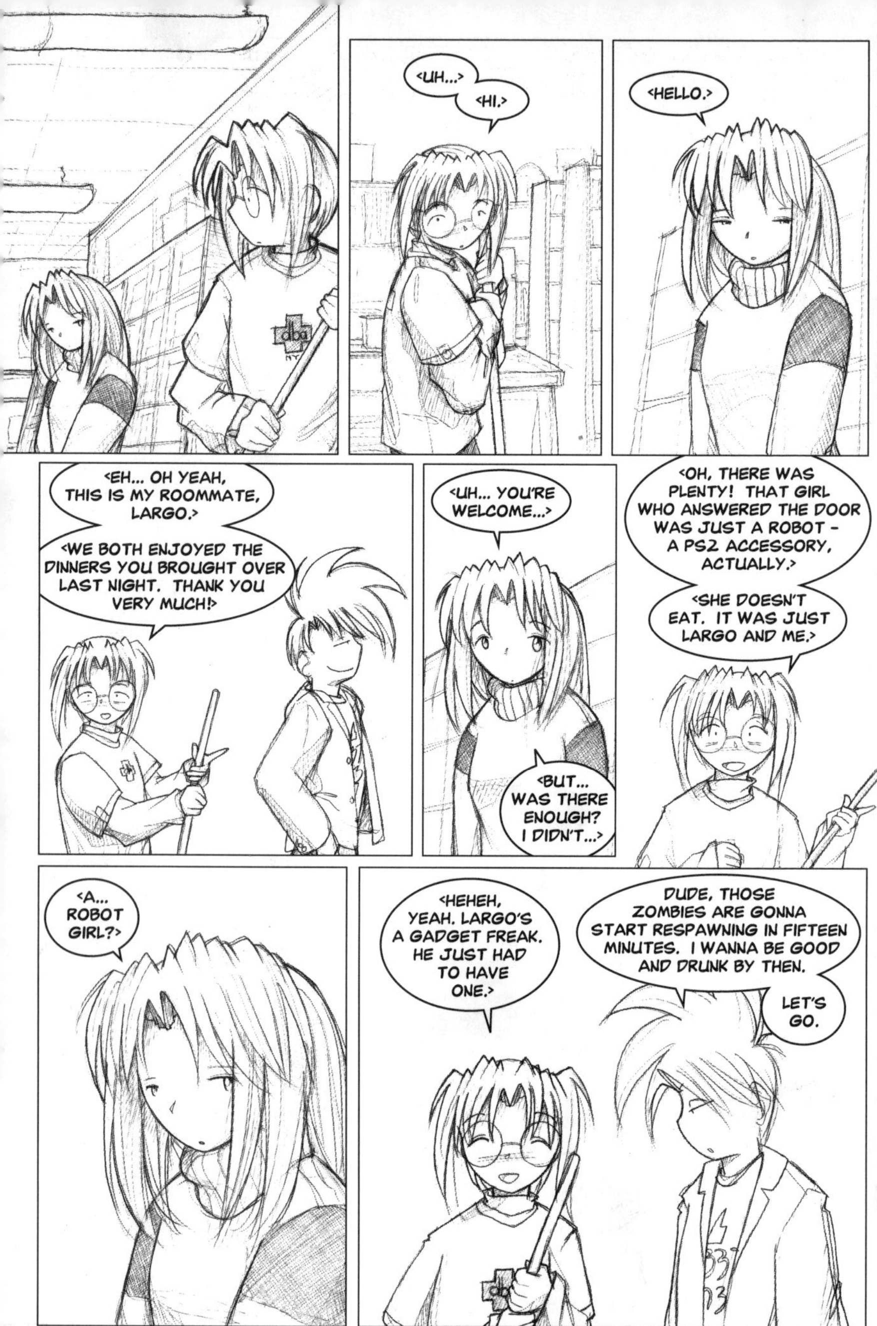
<UH...>
<HI.>
<HELLO.>
<EH... OH YEAH, THIS IS MY ROOMMATE, LARGO.>
<WE BOTH ENJOYED THE DINNERS YOU BROUGHT OVER LAST NIGHT. THANK YOU VERY MUCH!>
<UH... YOU'RE WELCOME...>
<BUT... WAS THERE ENOUGH? I DIDN'T...>
<OH, THERE WAS PLENTY! THAT GIRL WHO ANSWERED THE DOOR WAS JUST A ROBOT - A PS2 ACCESSORY, ACTUALLY.>
<SHE DOESN'T EAT. IT WAS JUST LARGO AND ME.>
<A... ROBOT GIRL?>
<HEHEH, YEAH. LARGO'S A GADGET FREAK. HE JUST HAD TO HAVE ONE.>
DUDE, THOSE ZOMBIES ARE GONNA START RESPAWNING IN FIFTEEN MINUTES. I WANNA BE GOOD AND DRUNK BY THEN.
LET'S GO.

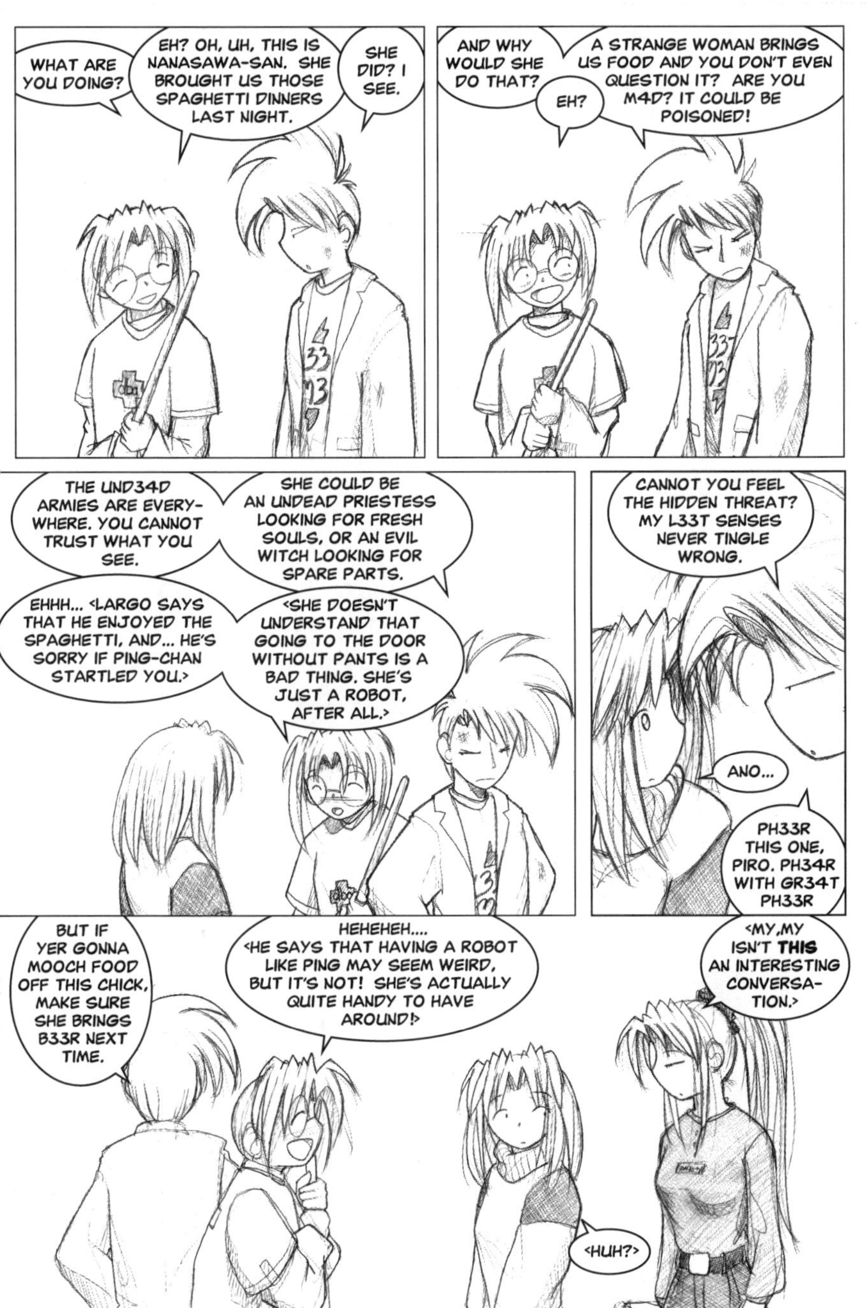
WHAT ARE YOU DOING?
EH? OH, UH, THIS IS NANASAWA-SAN. SHE BROUGHT US THOSE SPAGHETTI DINNERS LAST NIGHT.
SHE DID? I SEE.
AND WHY WOULD SHE DO THAT?
EH?
A STRANGE WOMAN BRINGS US FOOD AND YOU DON'T EVEN QUESTION IT? ARE YOU M4D? IT COULD BE POISONED!
THE UND34D ARMIES ARE EVERY-WHERE. YOU CANNOT TRUST WHAT YOU SEE.
SHE COULD BE AN UNDEAD PRIESTESS LOOKING FOR FRESH SOULS, OR AN EVIL WITCH LOOKING FOR SPARE PARTS.
EHHH... <LARGO SAYS THAT HE ENJOYED THE SPAGHETTI, AND... HE'S SORRY IF PING-CHAN STARTLED YOU.>
<SHE DOESN'T UNDERSTAND THAT GOING TO THE DOOR WITHOUT PANTS IS A BAD THING. SHE'S JUST A ROBOT, AFTER ALL.>
CANNOT YOU FEEL THE HIDDEN THREAT? MY L33T SENSES NEVER TINGLE WRONG.
ANO...
PH33R THIS ONE, PIRO. PH34R WITH GR34T PH33R
BUT IF YER GONNA MOOCH FOOD OFF THIS CHICK, MAKE SURE SHE BRINGS B33R NEXT TIME.
HEHEHEH.... <HE SAYS THAT HAVING A ROBOT LIKE PING MAY SEEM WEIRD, BUT IT'S NOT! SHE'S ACTUALLY QUITE HANDY TO HAVE AROUND!>
<MY,MY ISN'T **THIS** AN INTERESTING CONVERSA-TION.>
<HUH?>

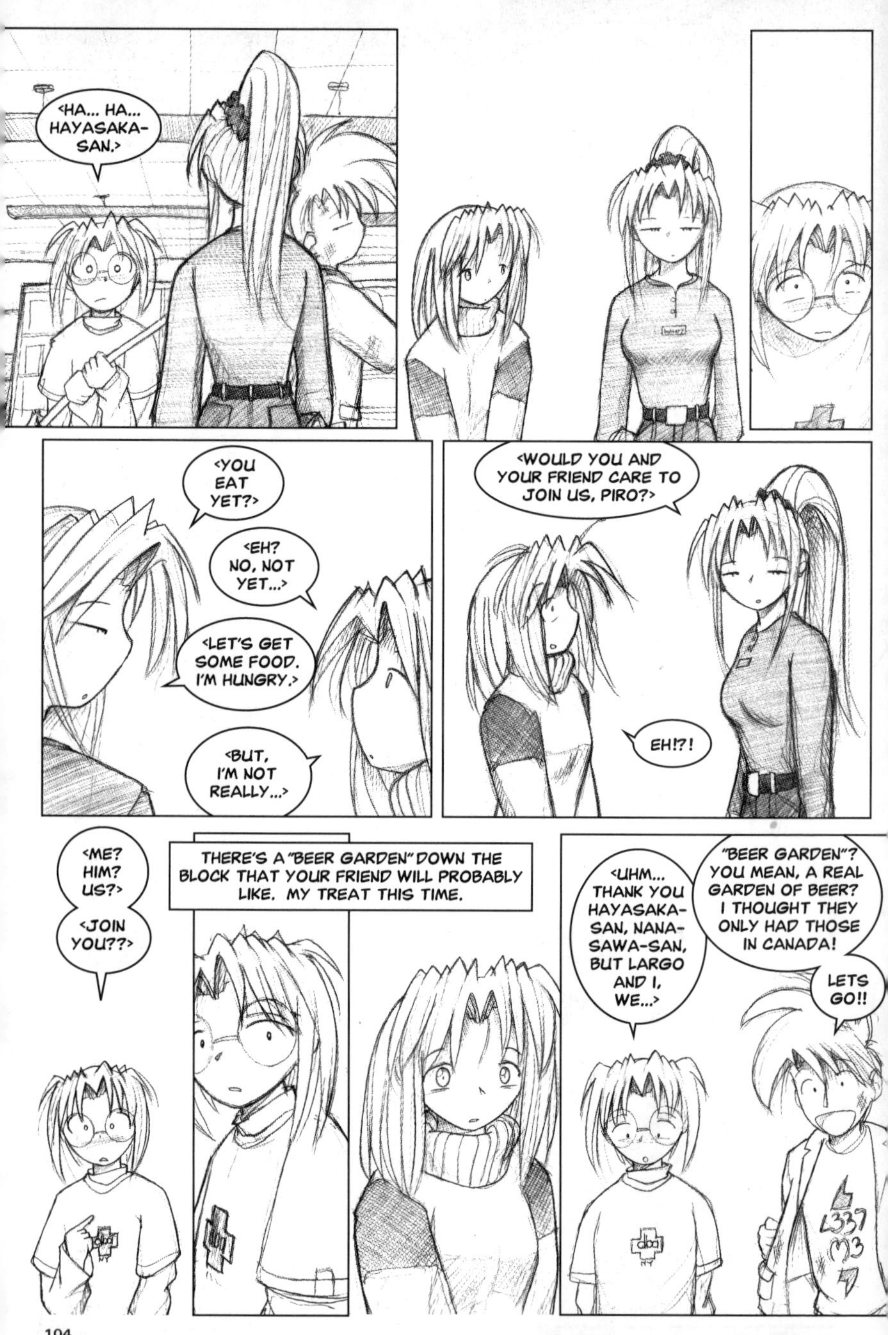
<HA... HA... HAYASAKA-SAN.>
<YOU EAT YET?>
<EH? NO, NOT YET...>
<LET'S GET SOME FOOD. I'M HUNGRY.>
<BUT, I'M NOT REALLY...>
<WOULD YOU AND YOUR FRIEND CARE TO JOIN US, PIRO?>
EH!?!
<ME? HIM? US?>
<JOIN YOU??>
THERE'S A "BEER GARDEN" DOWN THE BLOCK THAT YOUR FRIEND WILL PROBABLY LIKE. MY TREAT THIS TIME.
<UHM... THANK YOU HAYASAKA-SAN, NANA-SAWA-SAN, BUT LARGO AND I, WE...>
"BEER GARDEN"? YOU MEAN, A REAL GARDEN OF BEER? I THOUGHT THEY ONLY HAD THOSE IN CANADA!
LETS GO!!
L337 M3

<TOHYA-SAN?>
<YES?>
<PROMISE ME YOU WON'T GET SICK AGAIN WITHOUT TELLING ME?>

<HUH?>
<PROMISE!!>
<WHY?>

<BECAUSE WE'RE FRIENDS.>

<AND I DON'T WANT YOU TO BE ALL ALONE AGAIN.>
<PROMISE?>
<...>
<PROMISE!!>
<OK... I PROMISE.>

WAS THAT A PROGRAMMED RESPONSE? PART OF HER MEDICAL SYSTEM? SHE SEEMS SO... EARNEST.
FOR A MACHINE, SHE'S VERY CON-VINCING.
IT'S ALMOST LIKE HER FEELINGS ARE REAL...
AND HER'S TO GIVE.

IS SHE PLAYING WITH ME NOW? NO ONE HAS USED HER FOR WHAT SHE WAS MADE FOR, YET SHE SEEMS TO BE IMPROVISING...
ARE HER EMOTIVE PROCESSES THAT... REALISTIC?
I WONDER...
COULD SHE FILL MY NEEDS?

<PING-CHAN, WOULD YOU LIKE TO COME OVER AND VISIT MY PLACE TONIGHT?>

AMAZING. THEY'VE ALREADY REBUILT THIS ENTIRE AREA.
REBUILT?
YEP. THIS PART OF THE CITY WAS LEVELED JUST A FEW HOURS AGO.
OH?
THE UNDEAD ARMIES...
THEY CAME TO DESTROY...
IT STARTED WITH WHAT WE THOUGHT WAS AN EARTHQUAKE...
DOM! LOOK OUT THE WINDOW! WHAT'S THAT??
MY GOD, THAT'S ED!*
*NOTE: DOM HAD SLIPPED A TRACKING DEVICE ON ED'S CLOTHING EARLIER.
THIS SAYS THAT HE'S MOVING AT LEAST 100 METERS PER SECOND!
GPS SAYS HE'S HEADING RIGHT FOR A NATURAL GAS STORAGE FACILITY...
WHUMP!
OOPS.
THE SKY IS BURNING!! THIS IS SO FSKING COOL!!
THE ORDINANCE IN HIS BAG MUST HAVE EXPLODED ON IMPACT.
LITTLE DID WE KNOW THAT THE EXPLOSION ED'S IMPACT CAUSED WOULD UNLEASH UNSPEAKABLE HORRORS...

ALL WE COULD DO WAS WATCH AS THE HORROR UNFOLDED...
I'LL CALL THE VAN, IT'S CIRCLING THE BLOCK ON REMOTE.
DOM, LOOK.
OVER WHERE ED EX- PLODED!
UP IN THE SKY!
IT'S RAINING ZOMBIES!!
THE EXPLOSION ED SET OFF MUST HAVE FORMED AN INTER- DIMENSIONAL RIFT.
WE'VE DUPLICATED THIS IN THE SEGA LABS BEFORE - IT'S WHERE THE SEGA CD CAME FROM.
I'VE GOT A BAD FEELING ABOUT--
NO! NOT THAT OVERUSED QUOTE!
FINISH THAT SENTENCE AND I'LL SHOOT YOU.
BESIDES...
-CHIRP- -CHIRP-
I'M ACTUALLY FEELING PRETTY GOOD RIGHT NOW.
WOW! A REAL BLACK OPS MINIVAN!!! SW33T!!
KINDA GIVE'S YA THE WARM FUZZIES, DOESN'T IT?
SEGA BLACK GEMA OPS
WOOSH!!!
skr33ch!
PRETTY MUCH EVERYTHING WE NEED. START GRABBING.
HMMM.
EVEN WITH DOM'S VAN FULL OF SPECIAL EQUIPMENT, WE STILL FACED IMPOSSIBLE ODDS. HOW COULD WE POSSIBLY DESTROY AN ENTIRE UNDEAD ARMY?
OF COURSE, IF DOM HAD ANY CROSSBOWS IT'D BE EASY, BUT DOM ONLY LIKES WEAPONS WITH EXPLOSIVE PROJECTILES.
I DON'T REALLY KNOW HIM. HE JUST FOLLOWED ME HOME ONE DAY...

HERE WE ARE.
BEER-GARDEN "SEA OF ILLUMINATION". IT'S ON THE ROOF.
SWEET!
<WELCOME TO BEERGARDEN> "HIKARI NO UMI", <WHAT CAN I GET FOR YOU TONIGHT?>
OHH... THEY HAVE THE **BIG** MUGS HERE!
<THREE MUGS AND ONE "ALL YOU CAN DRINK" SPECIAL.>
<BRING US SOME APPE-TIZERS TOO.>
WOW! THIS PLACE IS FAST! MY B33R IS H33R!
OHH... N3KTAR OF THE GODZ...
GLUG GLUG GLUG GLUG
-GLURK-
AHHH...
A LITTLE WATERED DOWN, BUT STILL, A FINE VINTAGE. I NEED ANOTHER ONE TO MAKE SURE.
SO, DID YOU ACTUALLY TASTE ANY OF THAT?

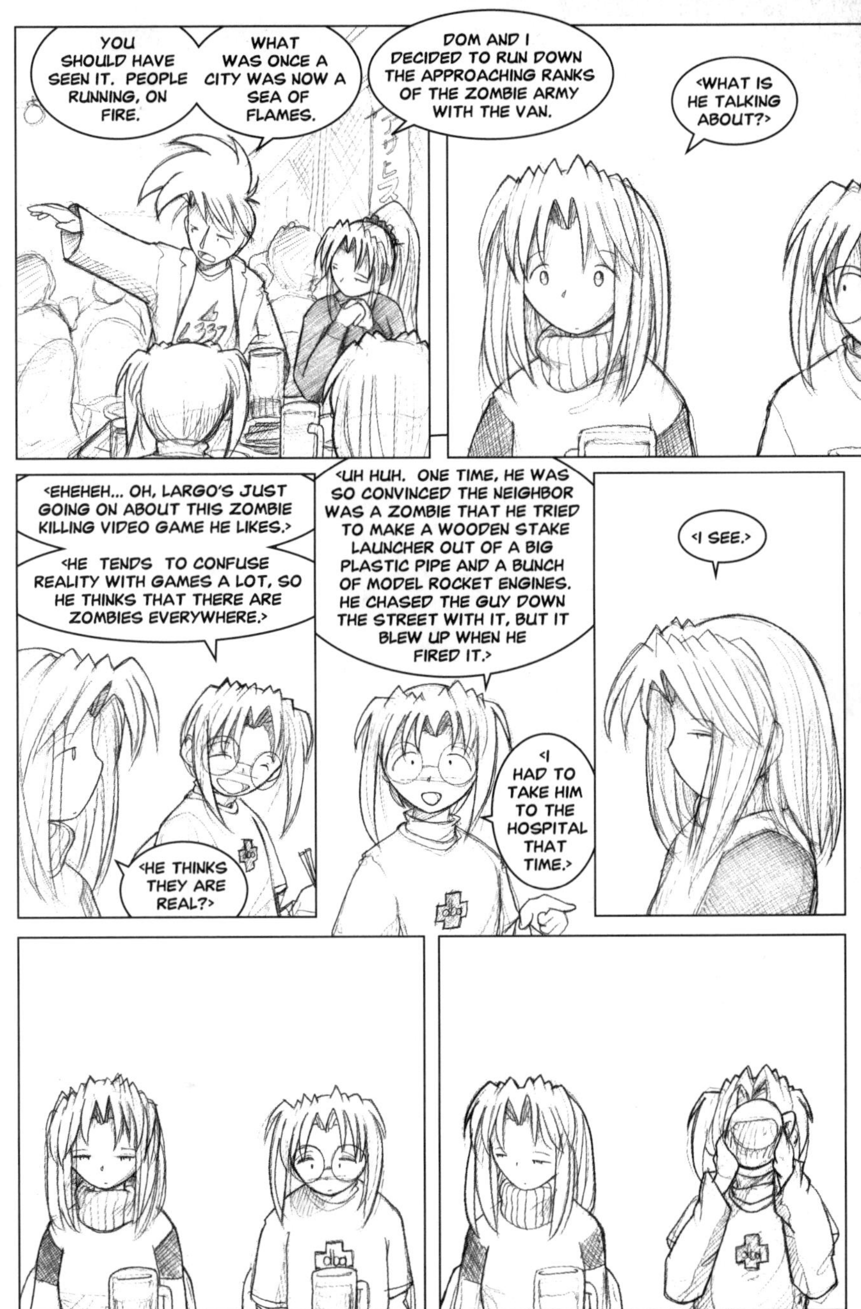
YOU SHOULD HAVE SEEN IT. PEOPLE RUNNING, ON FIRE.
WHAT WAS ONCE A CITY WAS NOW A SEA OF FLAMES.
DOM AND I DECIDED TO RUN DOWN THE APPROACHING RANKS OF THE ZOMBIE ARMY WITH THE VAN.
L337
<WHAT IS HE TALKING ABOUT?>
<EHEHEH... OH, LARGO'S JUST GOING ON ABOUT THIS ZOMBIE KILLING VIDEO GAME HE LIKES.>
<HE TENDS TO CONFUSE REALITY WITH GAMES A LOT, SO HE THINKS THAT THERE ARE ZOMBIES EVERYWHERE.>
<HE THINKS THEY ARE REAL?>
<UH HUH. ONE TIME, HE WAS SO CONVINCED THE NEIGHBOR WAS A ZOMBIE THAT HE TRIED TO MAKE A WOODEN STAKE LAUNCHER OUT OF A BIG PLASTIC PIPE AND A BUNCH OF MODEL ROCKET ENGINES. HE CHASED THE GUY DOWN THE STREET WITH IT, BUT IT BLEW UP WHEN HE FIRED IT.>
<I HAD TO TAKE HIM TO THE HOSPITAL THAT TIME.>
<I SEE.>

WE RODE DOWN THE UNDEAD LEGIONS UNTIL WE COULD GO NO FURTHER...
EWW, ZOMBIE FUNK.
<COULD YOU PASS THE SOY SAUCE, PLEASE?>
<UHM, SURE THING.>
DAMN ZOMBIES, SCRATCHING THE CLEAR COAT...
BLAM!
BLAM!
URK!
<SO...>
<YOU'RE A VOICE ACTRESS?>
<NOT REALLY.>
<I ONCE HAD A ROLE IN A SMALL, CHEAP, UN-REMARKABLE GAME.>
<I'D HARDLY CALL IT A CAREER.>
RESISTANCE WAS FIERCE, BUT WITH MASSIVE FIREPOWER AT OUR DISPOSAL, WE WERE ABLE TO MAKE SHORT WORK OF THE REMAINING ZOMBIES.
I PH34R NO GIB!
BLAM! BLAM!
GET ME AN AIR FRESHENER.
<I DON'T THINK I REALLY WANT TO BE ONE ANYMORE.>
<IT SEEMS I'M ONLY GOOD ENOUGH FOR CHEAP FANTASIES.>
BUT WE WERE UNPREPARED FOR WHAT AWAITED US...
OOOOHHH... WHAT'S THIS?
LARGO!! DON'T TOUCH THAT! IT'S...

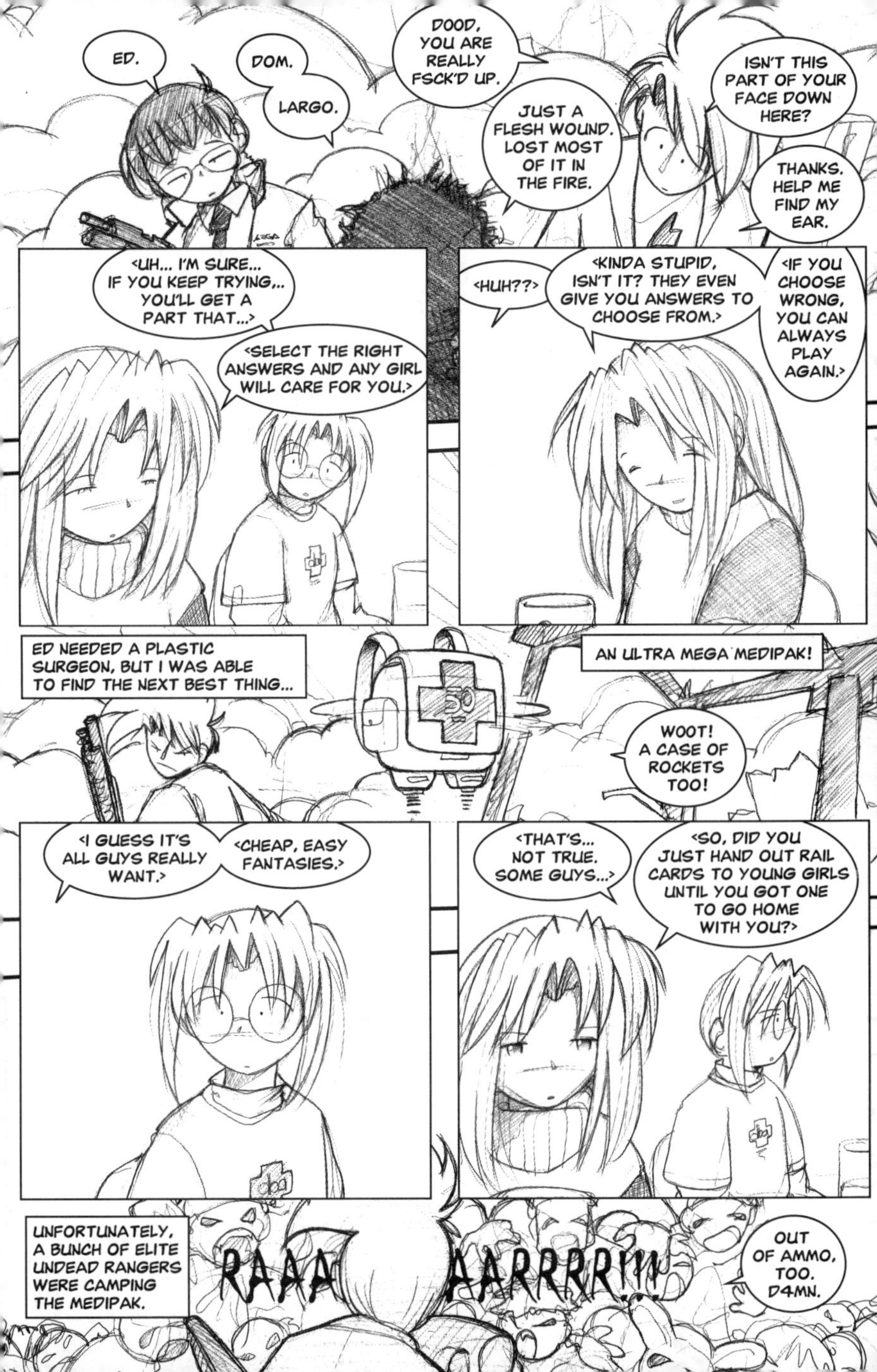

ED.
DOM.
LARGO.
DOOD, YOU ARE REALLY FSCK'D UP.
JUST A FLESH WOUND. LOST MOST OF IT IN THE FIRE.
ISN'T THIS PART OF YOUR FACE DOWN HERE?
THANKS. HELP ME FIND MY EAR.
<UH... I'M SURE... IF YOU KEEP TRYING,.. YOU'LL GET A PART THAT...>
<SELECT THE RIGHT ANSWERS AND ANY GIRL WILL CARE FOR YOU.>
<HUH??>
<KINDA STUPID, ISN'T IT? THEY EVEN GIVE YOU ANSWERS TO CHOOSE FROM.>
<IF YOU CHOOSE WRONG, YOU CAN ALWAYS PLAY AGAIN.>
ED NEEDED A PLASTIC SURGEON, BUT I WAS ABLE TO FIND THE NEXT BEST THING...
AN ULTRA MEGA MEDIPAK!
WOOT! A CASE OF ROCKETS TOO!
<I GUESS IT'S ALL GUYS REALLY WANT.>
<CHEAP, EASY FANTASIES.>
<THAT'S... NOT TRUE. SOME GUYS...>
<SO, DID YOU JUST HAND OUT RAIL CARDS TO YOUNG GIRLS UNTIL YOU GOT ONE TO GO HOME WITH YOU?>
UNFORTUNATELY, A BUNCH OF ELITE UNDEAD RANGERS WERE CAMPING THE MEDIPAK.
RAAA AARRRRR!!!
OUT OF AMMO, TOO. D4MN.

EMPTY!
JAMMED!!
THAT THE END
WAS N3AR
THE HORROR BEGAN
<WHU...?
I PULLED OUT MY
SECRET WEAPON...
HAHAHAH!!!
PH34R MY SECRET
WEAPON OF ULTIMATE
DESTRUCTION!!!
PH34R MY

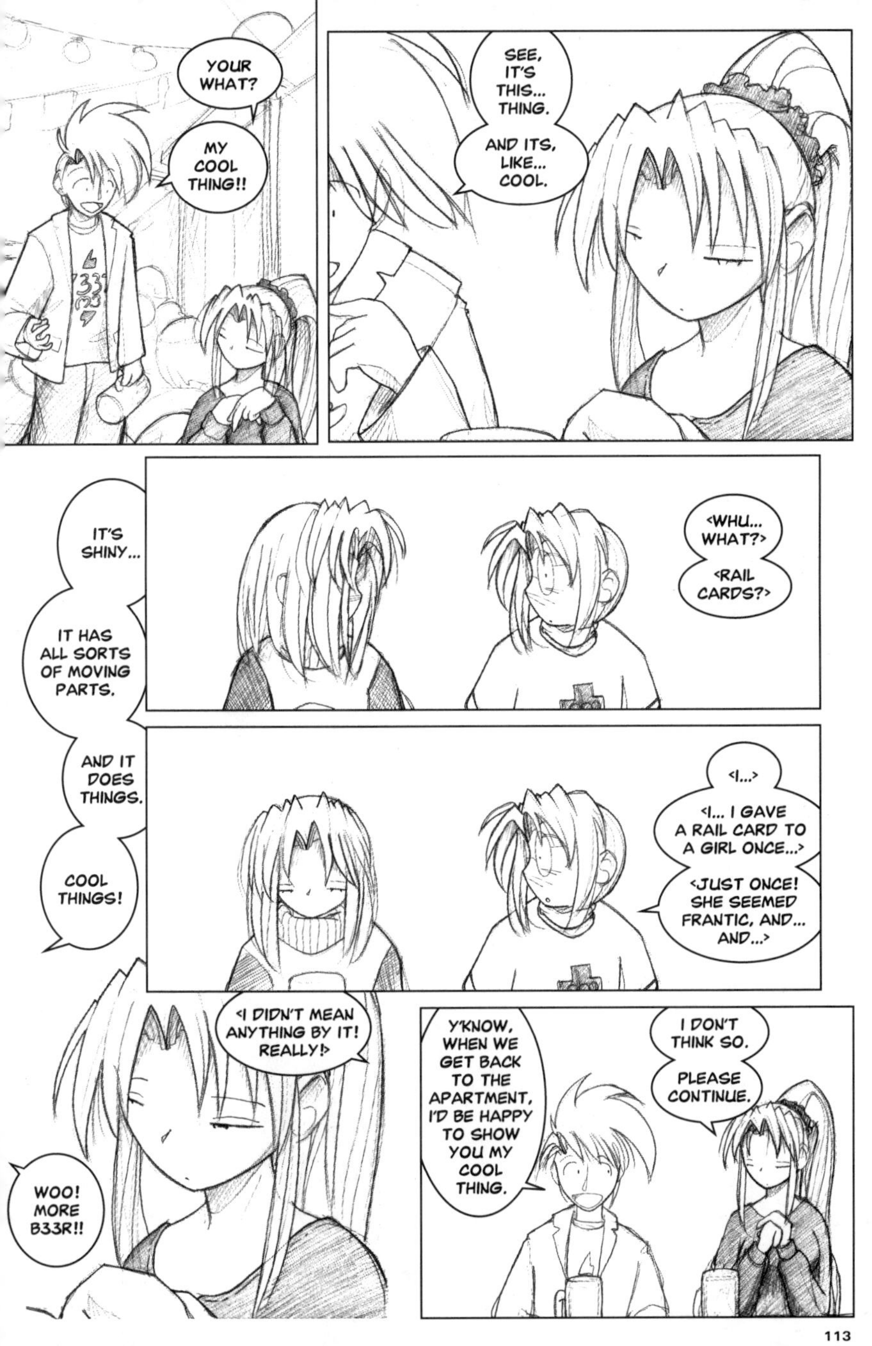
YOUR WHAT?
MY COOL THING!!
SEE, IT'S THIS... THING.
AND ITS, LIKE... COOL.
IT'S SHINY...
IT HAS ALL SORTS OF MOVING PARTS.
<WHU... WHAT?>
<RAIL CARDS?>
AND IT DOES THINGS.
COOL THINGS!
<I...>
<I... I GAVE A RAIL CARD TO A GIRL ONCE...>
<JUST ONCE! SHE SEEMED FRANTIC, AND... AND...>
<I DIDN'T MEAN ANYTHING BY IT! REALLY!>
WOO! MORE B33R!!
Y'KNOW, WHEN WE GET BACK TO THE APARTMENT, I'D BE HAPPY TO SHOW YOU MY COOL THING.
I DON'T THINK SO.
PLEASE CONTINUE.

FORTUNATELY, I AM ALWAYS PREPARED FOR SITUATIONS LIKE THIS.
ack!
my baaaag... my baa-aagg!!!
rowr, yo.
<I DON'T UNDERSTAND WHY YOU'RE SO MAD AT ME.>
<SO I HAVE A PS2 ROBOT GIRL. NEVER USED IT, SHE'S A FRIENDS.>
<SOME GIRL WANTS DRAWIN' LESSONS. I TRY TO GET OUT OF IT, BUT YOUR ROOMMATE BUTTS IN.>
B3HOLD!! MY COOL THING!!
WITH THIS I CAN SUMMON A POWER GREATER THAN HELL ITSELF!!!
COME FORTH, MY PH34RBOT ARMIES!!!
COOL THING, LEND ME YOUR L33TNESS...
<I GIVE SOME GIRL MY RAILCARD, AND YOU THINK I'M SOME KIND OF SUBWAY PERVERT OR SOMETHIN.>
<THAT'S NOT FAIR. I HAD TO WALK ALL THE WAY BACK TO...>
NNHNNNNNHNNNNHNNH
PH34R BOT
NNHNHNNNHNNNHNN
CRUSH THE UNDEAD SWARM!!!!
<WH... WHAITA-MINUTE.>
<HOW'D YOU KNOW ABOUT THE RAILCARD THING?>
I DUN EVEN THINK I TOLD LARGO 'BOUT THAT...
rWaaaaaawrr!!!
TWEEEEEEEEEEEEEEEEEEFF!!
STOPPU

POLICE
<THIS IS INSPECTOR SONODA OF THE TOKYO POLICE CATACLYSM DIVISION. CEASE ALL DESTRUCTIVE ACTIVITIES AT ONCE.>
<I REPEAT, CEASE ALL DESTRUCTION OF PRIVATE PROPERTY IMMEDIATELY.>
<TH... THAT WAS YOU?>
<YOU WERE THE ONE THAT...??>
<YOU DON'T EVEN REMEMBER.>
<DOESN'T MATTER.>
<LIKE YOU SAID, IT DIDN'T MEAN ANYTHING.>
I WASN'T SURE WHAT WAS GOING ON, SINCE THE POLICEMAN WAS TALKING TO THE ZOMBIE IN IT'S OWN EVIL LANGUAGE.
<WELL, YOUR PAPERS ARE IN ORDER, BUT THIS RAMPAGE PERMIT IS FOR NEXT TUESDAY. YOU'RE A WEEK EARLY.>
<ROWRL? WRRRL...>
<YES, I'M GIVING YOU A TICKET. NEXT TIME VERIFY THE DAY THE PERMIT IS PULLED FOR **BEFORE** YOU RAMPAGE.>
<HERE.>
<500 YEN SHOULD COVER WHAT I USED.>
<WHAT? WHA-D'YA...?>
<I DON'T WANT IT.>
<HM, A FOREIGNER.>
I SEE NO MENTION OF OPPOSING FORCES ON THIS RAMPAGE PERMIT.
CAN I SEE YOUR PAPERS PLEASE?

BAM!
<SORRY...>
<TH... THANK YOU.>
<SORRY.>
KLON
<WHY DUZ THIS HAPPEN TO ME?>
<I MEET A GIRL I LIKE AND IT GETZ ALL SCREWED UP 'N I DUN EVEN KNOW WHUTI-DIDWRONG......>
<THIZ ALWAYZ HAPPENZ ITSNOT FAIR...>

SO, YOU WERE ARRESTED?
YEAH. THE COP WAS REALLY PISSED THAT I DIDN'T HAVE THE RIGHT PAPERWORK.
WASN'T A BIG DEAL.
JUNPEI WAS ABLE TO GET A RENT-A-ZILLA ON SHORT NOTICE AND BUST ME OUT AGAIN.
REALLY.
PIRO'S SUCH A LIGHTWEIGHT.
SHAME TO WASTE GOOD BEER ON THE WUSS.
PIRO DOESN'T DRINK OFTEN?
NAH. HE ONLY LIQUORS UP AND GETS ALL WEEPY OVER CHIXOR.
DOESN'T HAPPEN THAT OFTEN.
LEAST HE AIN'T AS FAT AS THE LAST TIME I HAD TO HAUL HIS DRUNK A55 HOME.
WOAH...
YOU ARE **R4CK3D!**
HEY, BOTH OF OUR ROOMIES ARE TOTALLY WASTED.
WHADDYA SAY...
WHEN WE GET TO YOUR PLACE LET ME SHOW YOU WHAT L33T THINGS I CAN DO WITH YOUR SYSTEMZ.
I KIN MAK3 EM SCR34M!
HMHMF HMFHUMF?
DID I HEAR A SCREAM OF "ULTIMATE SUFFERING"?
I THINK THAT'S ALL IN YOUR HEAD, ED.

HNNNG...
breeeeep. breeeeeep. breeeeep.
HOW'D I GET BACK HERE...
THE 3VIL DEVICE BECKONS...
breeeeeep!
HUWA? WHERE'D YOU GET A CELL PHONE?
SHHHH!
breeeeep.
breeeeeep.
HELLO?
WHAT HAPPENED TO YOUR ARM?
YES.
YES.
IT'S FOR YOU.
HUH? FOR ME?
<I GUESS YOU DON'T CARE ABOUT ME AFTER ALL, DO YOU, PIRO-NIISAN?>

<WHA? PING, WHERE ARE YOU? WHERE?>
WHAT A WUSS.
<HUH? BUT I DIDN'T... NO, I WASN'T...>
LOOK AT THAT. APOLOGIZING TO A COMPUTER GAME.
WHAT HAVE YOU DONE TO THE POOR SAP?
OH, AS IF YOUR ADVICE WOULDN'T MAKE HIM WORSE.

PAH. FIRST OFF, HE NEEDS TO RESET THAT PS2 DOLL AND MAKE IT SERVE HIS NEEDS. THEN THERE'S A STORE FULL OF GAMES HE CAN SINK HIMSELF INTO.
BETTER THAN THE MISERY YOU'VE SET HIM UP FOR.

IS ALL THAT COLOGNE MAKING YOU HIGH? STAY AWAY FROM HIM.
OH? YOU THINK YOU CAN STOP ME?
DON'T UNDERESTIMATE ME.

SOUNDS LIKE A CHALLENGE.
NAME THE TIME AND PLACE. PREFERABLY SOME-WHERE THAT'S WELL VENTILATED.

AS YOU WISH, PRISSYWINGS, THE ROOF, ONE HOUR.
I WON'T HOLD BACK!!

I WON'T HOLD BACK EITHER, ASMODEUS.

DEVIL & GROMMET PAKC-334 55MM ATROCITY RIFLE. CHECK.
LUCIF CGG626 "ANGEL-HAMMER" BFG. CHECK.
GOOL INDUSTRIES 320MM 'FLOWER-STOMPER". CHECK.
THIS? THIS IS YOUR 'PARTNER' WHO'S "FAR SEXIER" THAN ME??
IT'S A SHAME TO HAVE TO KILL YOU. I COULD HAVE SHOWN YOU A THING OR TWO.
BOO IS HERE MERELY TO OBSERVE.
AND I'D PREFER DEATH OVER ANYTHING YOU COULD POSSIBLY SHOW ME.
THE ONLY THING I WILL SHOW YOU IS YOUR DOOM!!
HEH.
POINK
-SCREEEEECH-
DON'T BE AFRAID TO TAKE ADVANTAGE OF YOUR ENEMY'S WEAKNESSES,
BECAUSE WINNING IS EVERYTHING, AFTER ALL.
N... NO FAIR...
SQUEEK!

<SINCE SHE FIRST MET SUGIYAMA-SAN ON THAT COLD, SNOWY, WINTER DAY, MANY THINGS HAD HAPPENED, BUT VERY LITTLE HAD ACTUALLY CHANGED.>
<YET MICHIKO WAS SURE OF ONE THING. SOMETHING HAD CHANGED IN HIS HEART.>
<JUST A LITTLE...>
<AND THAT WAS ENOUGH FOR NOW.>
END CHAPTER 2

HAH! NOW YOU DIE!! PREPARE TO SUCK PLAZMA!
-click-
WOOT. HEADSHOT.
BATTERIES DIE IN YOUR CORDLESS KEYBOARD AGAIN, LARGO?
DIE! DIE! DIE!!
BIT3
STOMP STOMP STOMP

megat
IN TODAY'S EPISODE OF "LEAVE IT TO SERAPHIM!" WE TAKE A BEHIND THE SCENES LOOK AT HOW WE PREPARE FOR EACH EPISODE OF *MEGATOKYO*.
IT'S NOT ALL FUN AND GAMES!
leave it to seraphim!

I ARRIVE AT THE SET EARLY EVERY MORNING.
IT'S USUALLY SEVERAL HOURS BEFORE MY SCENE.
THERE ARE A LOT OF STEPS TO GO THROUGH BEFORE I AM READY FOR THE CAMERA.

FIRST, THERE'S HAIR AND MAKEUP. AN ESSENTIAL STEP FOR ALL CAST MEMBERS.
WOW, THE CIRCLES UNDER YOUR EYES ARE GETTING HUGE!
YOU'RE FIRED.

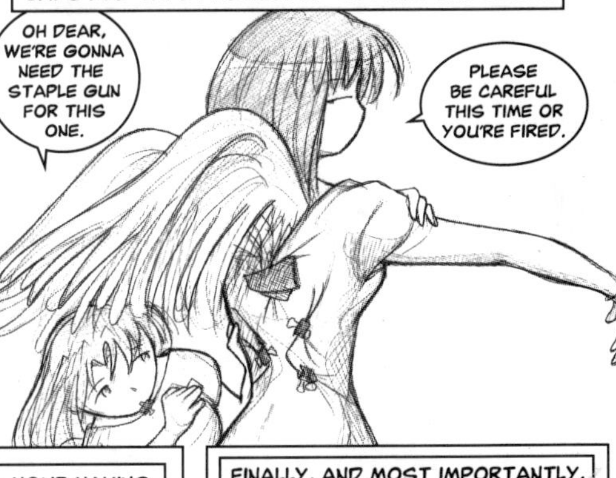
NEXT IS WARDROBE. IT'S NOT EASY GETTING OFF THE RACK TO FIT LIKE DESIGNER WEAR, ESPECIALLY WHEN YOU ARE SUPER EXTRA PETITE. A LOT OF CLIPS AND TAPE ARE NEEDED TO MAKE THINGS FIT.
OH DEAR, WE'RE GONNA NEED THE STAPLE GUN FOR THIS ONE.
PLEASE BE CAREFUL THIS TIME OR YOU'RE FIRED.

I HAVE TO SPEND AT LEAST AN EXTRA HOUR HAVING MY WINGS STYLED AND ARRANGED. EVERY FEATHER MUST BE IN PLACE BEFORE I CAN DO MY SCENE.
PULL ANOTHER FEATHER OUT AND YOU'RE BOTH FIRED.
IT'S NOT LIKE YOU CAN JUST GLUE THEM BACK ON.
MEGATOKYO

FINALLY, AND MOST IMPORTANTLY, WE GET TO DIGITAL ENHANCEMENT. HERE, ANY IMPERFECTION OR FLAW CAN BE MADE TO MAGICALLY DISAPPEAR...
DON'T FORGET TO ERASE MY TATTOO OR YOU'RE FIRED.
YES MA'M.

Shirt_Guy_Dom.txt

Ever since starting *Megatokyo*, one thing hasn't changed – I've been struggling to get ahead. So far I haven't managed it.

One of the problems with an online webcomic is that there is little incentive to really finish them more than a few minutes before they go online. The Monday, Wednesday, Friday schedule is more of a goal than something strictly adhered to. As many *Megatokyo* readers know, there are times when I miss a comic or two. Even so, I always try to have SOMETHING to put up in it's place.

Of all the things I can put up in place of a missing strip the worst is a Shirt Guy Dom comic.

What is a Shirt Guy Dom comic? I'm not really sure where they come from, nor do I really want to know. All I do know is that they involve a trackball, Dom's twisted way of looking at things, chopped up bits and pieces of existing *MT* comics, and access to the website to upload the finished … strip.

That said, I think Shirt Guy Dom comics have at least one redeeming quality -- they help readers appreciate the comics I do that much more. I've discovered that the mere threat of a SGD comic is enough to quiet even the most vocal critic.

If the horror is too much to bear, please note that the following pages are part of a convenient pull out section.

THOUGHT YOU'D ESCAPED, DIDN'T YOU? WELL, THINK AGAIN. PIRO HAS WRITER'S BLOCK. IT'S EASY TO WRITE THIS CRAP, SO: ONCE AGAIN, DOM PRESENTS...
NAZE NANI SHIRT GUY DOM!
IT'S BEEN A LONG TIME, MEAT PUPPETS. A LOT HAS HAPPENED SINCE I DID A FILL-IN, HASN'T IT?
PEOPLE HAVE CHANGED. PLOTS HAVE ADVANCED. BUT ONE THING REMAINS UNCHANGED HERE AT MT.
(THIS IS A FENCE)
OKAY, TWO THINGS HAVE REMAINED UNCHANGED. SILLY COSTUMES, AND THE FACT THAT DOM IS ONE CRAZY MOTHER--
THE SILLY COSTUMES.
SHUT YOUR MOUTH!
I WAS JUST TALKING ABOUT MYSELF!
I CAN DIG IT.
(IT IS NOT THE FENCE THAT BENDS, IT IS YOU THAT BENDS.)
(SHNOOGINS.)
ANYWAY, WHAT I WANTED TO SAY BEFORE I WAS SO RUDELY INTERRUPTED IS THAT JUST LIKE THE OTHERS, I HAVE MY OWN DISTORTED VISION OF REALITY. LET'S TAKE A LOOK THROUGH MY EYES. ONE OTAKON EVENT AT A TIME.
[OTAKON REALITY: FRIDAY, AUGUST 10 5:00 PM]
IT'S BEEN A LONG DAY. WE SHOULD EAT SOON.
MT SHIRTS EVERYWHERE...
YELLOW DOM NEEDS FOOD BADLY!
(???)
(ME)
(LARGO)
(PIRO)
[DOM'S REALITY: SAME DATE]
TRAIN OF FANS TO ZONE!
HURRY, PIRO, THEY'RE GAINING ON US FAST!
WE'RE NOT GONNA MAKE IT! WE'RE ALL GONNA DIE!
FORGET ABOUT ME! SAVE YOURSELVES AND THE POSTERS!
B33R!
J00 4R3 SO L33T!
SIGN MY BRA!
(FANS)
[OTAKON REALITY: FRIDAY, AUGUST 10 6:00 PM; MT PANEL]
WELCOME TO THE PANEL. I'M PIRO, THIS IS WING ZERO, TO MY LEFT IS LARGO, AND UP IN FRONT IS DOM. HE'S NOT ALLOWED ON STAGE.
HEY DOM, DO SOMETHING FUNNY.
(WING ZERO)
SO FULL OF HATE!
(AUDIENCE LAUGHTER)
(AUDIENCE LAUGHTER)
[DOM'S REALITY]
AND, SINCE I CONTROL THE MEANS OF PRODUCTION, I SHALL OPPRESS THIS YOUNG WORKER INTO SERVING ME, FOR I AND CAPITALISM ARE VILE.
DANCE FOR US, PROLETARIAT PUPPET!
MY AGRARIAN UTOPIA WILL BE WATERED WITH YOUR FILTHY BLOOD, PIG-DOGS.
(AUDIENCE SINGING THE INTERNATIONALE)

(CONTINUED ON NEXT PAGE -->)

(CONTINUED FROM PREVIOUS PAGE...)

[OTAKON REALITY: SATURDAY, AUG 11 8:00 PM; HARD ROCK CAFE, BALTIMORE]
HEY DOM, DON'T LOOK NOW, BUT I THINK THAT GIRL LIKES YOU.
HUH?
HI! YOU'RE CUTE. I LIKE YOU. HERE'S MY PHONE NUMBER!
HUH? WHERE?
YOU'RE A BIG FAT LIAR, FRED.
DOM, YOU MAY BE THE DUMBEST MAN ALIVE.
HUH?
(DUMB)
(AMUSED)
(ABLE)
(NAME WITHHELD)

[DOM'S REALITY]
BLAH BLAH BLAH, MYART SUCKS, BLAH BLAH BLAH, MEREKAT'S BETTER THAN ME, BLAH BLAH SARAH.
BLAH BLAH BLAH KILL ED, BLAH BLAH NEVER GONNA SIGN UNDERWEAR AGAIN.
HI! YOU'RE FUNNY. WANT MY E-MAIL ADDRESS SO WE CAN JOKE AROUND?
SURE! I LOVE A GOOD JOKE.
BLA BLA MEREKAT DOES BETTER ART.

WELL, FAITHFUL READERS, THERE YOU HAVE IT, MY REALITY.
OTHERWISE KNOWN AS "DOM'S A DUMBASS."
I REALLY WISH YOU'D SHUT UP.
I KNOW.
(ALSO AMUSED)
(PUNCH THE ED, AND WIN $20!)

ANYWAY, NEXT TIME WE WILL PRESENT DOM AND ED'S STICK FIGURE DOJO!
HEY WAIT, WHAT HAPPENED TO THE PART WHERE YOU HUMPED HOT SOUP'S LEG?
... I DEMAND SILENCE!
THE PUBLIC HAS A RIGHT TO KNOW ABOUT THAT.
ALRIGHT, CHANGE OF PLANS. NEXT TIME, IS "ED AND VERY LARGE SYRINGES THEATER."
...I'LL BE GOOD. PLEASE DON'T SHOW ME THE SPINAL TAP AGAIN....
SEE YOU LATER! SAME DOM-TIME, SAME DOM-SITE
(WAVING GOODBYE)

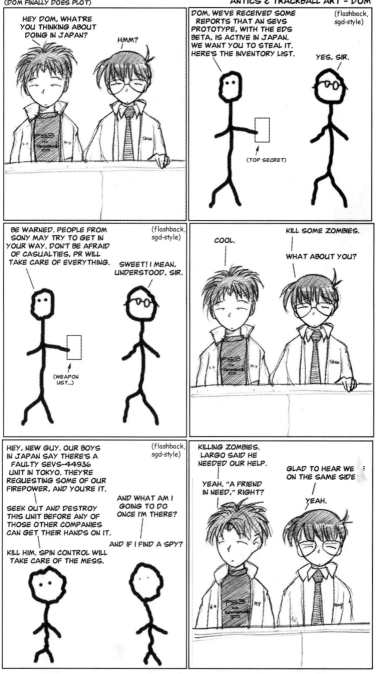

HEY DOM, WHAT'RE YOU THINKING ABOUT DOING IN JAPAN?
HMM?

(flashback, sgd-style)
DOM. WE'VE RECEIVED SOME REPORTS THAT AN SEVS PROTOTYPE, WITH THE EDS BETA, IS ACTIVE IN JAPAN. WE WANT YOU TO STEAL IT. HERE'S THE INVENTORY LIST.
YES, SIR.
(TOP SECRET)

(flashback, sgd-style)

BE WARNED. PEOPLE FROM SONY MAY TRY TO GET IN YOUR WAY. DON'T BE AFRAID OF CASUALTIES, PR WILL TAKE CARE OF EVERYTHING.

SWEET! I MEAN, UNDERSTOOD, SIR.

(WEAPON LIST...)

COOL.

KILL SOME ZOMBIES.

WHAT ABOUT YOU?

(flashback, sgd-style)

HEY, NEW GUY. OUR BOYS IN JAPAN SAY THERE'S A FAULTY SEVS-44936 UNIT IN TOKYO. THEY'RE REQUESTING SOME OF OUR FIREPOWER, AND YOU'RE IT.

AND WHAT AM I GOING TO DO ONCE I'M THERE?

SEEK OUT AND DESTROY THIS UNIT BEFORE ANY OF THOSE OTHER COMPANIES CAN GET THEIR HANDS ON IT.

AND IF I FIND A SPY?

KILL HIM. SPIN CONTROL WILL TAKE CARE OF THE MESS.

KILLING ZOMBIES. LARGO SAID HE NEEDED OUR HELP.
GLAD TO HEAR WE
ON THE SAME SIDE
YEAH. "A FRIEND IN NEED," RIGHT?
YEAH.

HEY KIDS! WANT TO KNOW WHAT GOES ON INSIDE OF DOM'S HEAD? NEITHER DO WE, BUT SINCE FRED'S BUSY AND DOM'S TRYING TO RECOVER FROM KATSUCON, YOU HAVE NO CHOICE. SO GET READY, BOYS AND GIRLS, BECAUSE MT PRESENTS:

JOURNEY TO THE CENTER OF DOM'S WEIRDNESS

MUHAHA.. AND WHO SAID TREPANNING WAS ONLY A PSEUDO-SCIENCE AT BEST?

(ED: NOT A LICENSED TREPANNER)

(CHISEL)

ZZZZ...

(TIRED AND SUFFERING FROM CON PLAGUE)

AS OUR FIRST STOP IN DOM'S NOGGIN, WE LOOK AT HIS VIEW OF MT'S FORUMS, AND ITS USERS.

I AM SET ADRIFT /
IN A SEA OF RABID FANS /
MY BRAIN HURTS SO MUCH.

ALL "MT = LOVE HINA" THREADS AND NO FAQ MAKE DOM GO SOMETHING SOMETHING...

...I WANT MY LIFE BACK.

(VIEWING LATEST "HAS ANYONE NOTICED MT IS A LOT LIKE LOVE HINA?" THREAD ON MT CENTRAL)

(TRYING HARD NOT TO CRY)

HMM. THAT DIDN'T GO TOO WELL. HOW ABOUT WE GO STRAIGHT TO HIS SEX DRIVE? THAT SHOULD BE PRETTY INTERESTING.

(SQUAT, UGLY, NON-PHALLIC SPECIES OF CACTUS)

(TUMBLEWEED)

NICE TRY, DOM. BUT YOU'RE NOT FOOLING ANYONE.

OKAY. OKAY. HIS HOPES AND DREAMS FOR THE FUTURE. THERE HAS TO BE SOME GOOD DIRT HERE.

HEY, WELCOME TO THE MEGATOKYO PANEL. I'M YOUR HOST, DOM, AND IN FRONT THERE IS PIRO. HEY, PIRO, DO SOMETHING ANGSTY. ANYWAY, THANK YOU ALL FOR SHOWING UP IN YOUR BOXERS--WE'LL BE ASSAULTING THE VIDEO ROOMS WITH DEODORANT AFTER THE PANEL, MY MOCK MAXIMO MINIONS..

SO FULL OF ANGST!

(OFF-SCREEN: ONE MILLION MAXIMOS)

(PIRO)

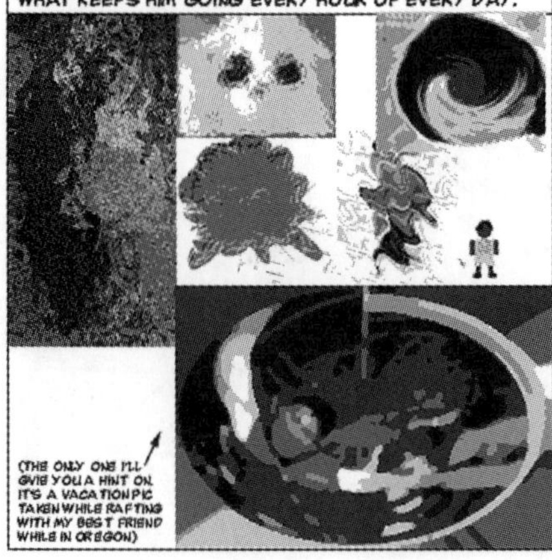

note: yes, i know, this comic looks "fuzzy". neither dom or i could find the original files.

FRED'S FAT'S IN THE FRYER, AND YOU ALL KNOW WHAT THAT MEANS--DOM DOES THE DIRTY WORK, AS ALWAYS... SO TODAY, IT'S
DOM ANSWERS DUMB QUESTIONS DAY

DOM AND ED HERE AGAIN. ON OUR DAY OFF, TOO.

I'M NOT EVEN SUPPOSED TO BE HERE TODAY!

(SHAKING FIST AT PIRO, THE OPPRES-SOR)

PIRO'S WARPED MIND IS BEYOND HUMAN KEN, SO WE DON'T BLAME YOU FOR ASKING QUESTIONS.

WE JUST WISH YOU'D BE QUIET FOR A FEW MINUTES AT A STRETCH.

ALRIGHT, SO QUESTION ONE: WHAT'S UP WITH MIHO? IS SHE GONNA DIE, OR WHAT?

THANKFULLY, THAT'S AN EASY ONE.

(PSST... THIS IS IMPORTANT)

SHE'S NOT DYING. SHE'S GOING TO ANOTHER DIMENSION.

BUT DON'T WORRY. SHE'LL EAT SOME MAGIC BEANS AND TRAIN, THEN COME BACK CUTER AND VILER THAN EVER.

NEXT QUESTION!

NEXT UP: IS LARGO REALLY THAT DUMB?

FOR THE ANSWER, WE DIRECT YOU TO THIS OLD PANEL--

ALL SHOULD BECOME CLEAR.

NO WAY THOSE ARE REAL. THEY CAN'T BE.

(RANDOM MAGICAL GIRL)

WHAT ABOUT YUKI? WHAT DOES SHE WANT FROM PIRO?

WHAT SHE REALLY WANTS TO DO IS FIGHT EVIL WITH THE MAGIC POWERS PIRO CAN GRANT HER.

UNFORTUNATELY, PIRO IS NOT A MAGICAL CAT, BUT A WHINY LOSER, SO THIS WILL NEVER COME TO PASS.

(SIAM-ESE CAT)

AND THE LAST QUESTION. IF ASMODEUS IS IN JAPAN, WHY AREN'T DOM AND ED?

WE CALL YOUR ATTENTION TO THE WINGS-AND TO THE FACT THAT HE DOESN'T EXIST.

AND ALSO NOTE THAT ED AND I ARE COMPLETELY FREE OF WINGS.

UM... DOM, THOSE FANGIRL NINJAS WOULD DISAGREE WITH YOU ON THAT ONE, I THINK...

HUH? WHAT DO YOU ME--AARGH!

(OFF-SCREEN: NATSUKI-LED NINJA HORDE)

WELL. UM, I GUESS THAT'S IT FOR NOW. SEE YOU NEXT TIME.

SWEET JESUS! HELP ME, ED! THEY'RE KILLING ME! IT BURNS...!

NO! NOT THE SPARKLES, ANYTHING BUT THE SPARKLES!

I REPENT! I'M SORRY! I DON'T KNOW WHAT I DID, BUT SORRY!

...OR NOT.

(SWEAT DROPLET)

(OFF-SCREEN: REVENGE FOR EVERY SGD EVER)

THAT'S RIGHT, FRED'S DEAD. LONG LIVE...
SHIRT GUY DOM'S CON REPORT
WELCOME TO MY REPORT OF HOW FANIME AND ACEN WENT, AT LEAST IN MY MIND.
ME? I'M HERE BECAUSE FRED'S AFRAID OF WHAT DOM MIGHT DO.
THAT REMINDS ME... BEFORE I DO THIS, I NEED TO GET BACK IN CHARACTER...
(ROLL OF DUCT TAPE)
PANTS? HEY, WAIT, WE'RE STICK FIGURES. I HAVE NO PANTS!
NO! BAD DOM! KEEP YOUR GODDAMN PANTS ON, FOR ONCE!
AWW, CHRIST... FRED! HELP ME! GET THE TAZER!
NUH UH, I'M NOT GETTING NEAR THAT. YOU'RE ON YOUR OWN.
(KING OF NO PANTS)
(WEARING PANTS, BY REQUEST)
O/~ AAALL WE HAVE TO DOO NOW... IS TAKE THESE PANTS, AND MAKE THEM FALL SOMEHOW! ALL WE HAVE TO SEE! IS THAT I GOT JUST ONE GREEN LEAF... AND YOU JUST GOT ONE GREEN LEAF, YEAH YEAH! FREEDOM, PULL MY PANTS RIGHT DOWN, FREEDOM, AND NEVER PULL THEM UP, FREEDOM! O/~
SOMEBODY HELP ME! HEY, YOU'RE HIS G--
WAH! PANTSLESS DOM SCARY! WAH!
(STILL WITHOUT PANTS. BUT IF I JUST HAVE ONE LEAF, IT'S OKAY)
(NO HELP FROM HERE)
OH! RIGHT, CON REPORT.
PART 1:
UH OH! ACEN'S IN TWO DAYS AND I DON'T HAVE A COSTUME READY!
HEY, WAIT. I'LL COSPLAY AS DOM! I ALREADY HAVE ALL THE PIECES, I'M ASIAN, I WEAR GLASSES...
(RANDOM CON-GOER)
EASIEST COSTUME EVER!
PART 2:
REMEMBER. IF YOU KILL YOURSELF, DO IT AWAY FROM THE HOTEL, FRED.
BUT... IT'S NOT EVEN SNOWING! I CAN'T GET MY ANGST ON IN THIS WEATHER!
(WHEE-OO HE LOOKS JUST LIKE BUDDY HOLLY...)
PART 3:
ALRIGHT, EVERYONE, IT'S TIME TO PLAY DOM'S FAVORITE GAME, "ROLL THE DRUNK ASMODEUS!"
HUH?
AUGH! GIVE ME BACK MY SHIRT, DOM! DAMN YOU!
(TWO LESSONS: 1) NEVER ACCEPT A DRINK FROM UKYO. 2) NEVER BE DRUNK AROUND DOM, WHO DOESN'T DRINK, BUT LIKES TO MESS WITH DRUNK PEOPLE.)
PART YATTA!
GOT YOUR LEAF, DOM?
YOU, ME, ED, A COUPLE OTHERS.
OF COURSE. WHO'S IN?
LET'S DO THIS!
THERE WILL BE NO YATTA IN THIS KARAOKE ROOM!
OFFENDERS WILL BE SHOT!
HENRY(?)
ME(?)
(MICROPHONE)
THAT'S ALL, FOLKS!

LITTLE DID WE KNOW THAT THE EXPLOSION ED'S IMPACT CAUSED WOULD UNLEASH UNSPEAKABLE HORRORS...

THE ORDNANCE IN
IS PACK MUST'VE EXPLODED ON
MPACT!

HEY, ISN'T THAT "TOKYO BIG SITE" OVER THERE?

GPS

SO WE RAN OVER TO GRAB ED (THE MYSTERY MACHINE BROKE DOWN SO WE COULDN'T DRIVE.)

HEY! WHAT'S THAT OVER BY ED, GANG?

JINKIES! IT LOOKS LIKE A HOLE IN THE FABRIC OF SPACE-TIME!

ZOIKS!

(DOM IN A"FRED" COSTUME - NOTE SWELL PANTS)

(VELMA. YES, THE REAL ONE. WE THINK.)

(LARGO DRESSED LIKE "SHAGGY" NOTE THE FUZZY CHIN.)

WE DIDN'T QUITE KNOW WHAT WAS GOING ON, BUT WE KNEW WE NEEDED GUNS. BIG GUNS. LOTS OF GUNS...

PING. LOAD UP THE "BLOW THINGS UP" PROGRAM.

WOAH.

DUAL BLACK BERETTAS

COMBAT SHOTGUN

SPNK-R ROCKET LAUNCHER

BUT IT WAS EASIER SAID THAN DONE.

GOOD GOD, THE RIFT'S SPEWING OUT HUNDREDS OF THEM!

THE STENCH... OVER-WHELMING...

WE FOUGHT FOR HOURS AGAINST A NEVER-ENDING HORDE OF MORBIDLY OBESE, SCANTILY CLAD COSPLAYING MEN. SUCH COSTUMES AS OTHER MEN SHOULD NEVER, EVER HAVE TO SEE...

<piro> uh, dom.
<dom> hey piro
<piro> what's this?
<dom> my proposal for largo's flashback sequence. I improved your weak sauce story.
*piro goes to look.
<piro> aghhh!! my eyes!!!
*piro jabs a pencil into each eye repeatedly.
<dom> I see that you like it better than my last one. here, let me finish that love scene...
<piro> for the love of civilization, will someone PLEASE TAKE THAT TRACKBALL AWAY FROM DOM!! AAAAAAGH!!!

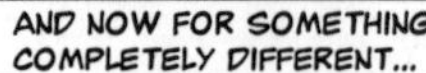
AND NOW FOR SOMETHING COMPLETELY DIFFERENT...

CRUD... I'VE COMPLETELY MESSED THINGS UP WITH KIMIKO. I WONDER WHAT I CAN DO NOW. I BET SHE HATES MY GUTS...
SHOULD I BUY HER DINNER? SHOULD I WAIT IN FRONT OF HER DOOR AND APOLOGIZE?
THIS IS ALWAYS SO MUCH EASIER IN DATING GAMES.
(PIRO)

THAT'S IT!
(LIGHT BULB)

DATING GAMES ALWAYS HAVE WALKTHROUGHS ON THE WEB SOMEWHERE. I JUST HAVE TO FIND THE ONE FOR KIMIKO! LET'S SEE... SEARCH FOR... <KIMIKO EVENT MEGATOKYO>.
GOT IT! BLESS YOU, GOOGLE.
NEGATIVE SPACE, I BANISH THEE!

TWO DAYS LATER: KIMIKO'S BIRTHDAY
<CHOCOLATE? FOR ME? UM. THANKS, PIRO-KUN. THAT'S SWEET OF YOU.>
<(NOW, WHAT'D THE WALKTHROUGH SAY TO DO? OH YEAH...)>
<(GOTTA WAIT FOR THE CHOICE TO POP UP, AND THEN...)>

1) <IT'S THE LEAST I CAN DO FOR SOMEONE AS KIND AND SWEET AS YOU ARE.>

2) <IT'S WHAT A MAN HAS TO DO FOR A GIRL HE'S MADLY IN LOVE WITH.>

3) <KIMIKO... I... YOU... UM. I KNEW IT, WORDS CAN'T EXPRESS MY FEELINGS...>

4) <I'M FATTENING YOU UP BEFORE I EAT YOU.>
<AH, THERE'RE THE CHOICES. AND ACCORDING TO THIS, THE KIMIKO++ CHOICE IS...>
4!

ONE MINUTE LATER:
JUST LIKE THE WALKTHROUGH SAID! A CG EVENT'N EVERYTHING!
IT HURTS... BUT AFTER HALLOWEEN IT'LL GET BETTER.

(BOX STUCK IN VERY UNCOMFORTABLE PART OF BODY)

ALRIGHT, SO THE CHOCOLATE BOX EVENT IS DONE. NEXT CG IS... HMM, I NEED TO THROW ROTTEN EGGS AT HER ON HALLOWEEN, AND CHOOSE <EGGS LOOK GOOD ON YOU>.

MEANWHILE, AT DOM'S PLACE
HE BOUGHT IT?
HOOK, LINE, AND SINKER.
SO WHAT'S THE PLAN?
KEEP UPDATING THE PAGE. I WANNA SEE IF WE CAN GET HIM TO LOOK UP HER SKIRT ON CHRISTMAS EVE.
...AND WHY ARE WE DOING THIS, EXACTLY?
BECAUSE I LIKE SEEING GROWN MEN WEEP.
FAIR ENOUGH.

"doko kana megatokyo!!"
WELCOME TO TODAY'S EPISODE OF "WHERE OH WHERE IS MEGATOKYO"
IT'S LIKE A COMIC THAT PRETENDS TO BE A REAL COMIC BY CREATIVELY RE-USING AND RE-EDITING FOOTAGE FROM PREVIOUS EPISODES.
WE FIGURE THAT ANYTHING IS BETTER THAN SHIRT GUY DOM DAYS.
largo l33t usagi
piro neko oniisan
I DUNNO ABOUT THAT.
YOU ARE KINDA OUT-LAME'ING DOM HERE.
QUIET, OR I WON'T TELL YOU WHERE I HID YOUR BEER.

IN TODAY'S "THE HOW AND WHY OF MEGATOKYO," WE ARE GOING TO TALK ABOUT HOW LARGO AND I DEAL WITH TROLLS AND FLAMES.
BANNING TROLLS CAN BE DULL AND TIRESOME, SO TO MAKE IT MORE EXCITING, I'VE ADDED A SPECIAL LITTLE SOMETHING TO OUR SERVER...
BEHOLD, WHACK-A-TROLL(TM)!!
WACK -A- TROLL!
BASICALLY, EVERY TIME YOU HIT ONE, IT BANS A RANDOM TROLL FROM THE SITE.
WHAT HAPPENS IF YOU HIT THAT BLUE TROLL?
SCOTT KURTZ GETS A WEDGIE.
DIE!
WHAM!
DIE!
WHAM!
DIE!
WHAM!
WEDGIE!!
WHAM!
DIE!
WHAM!
I USE A LESS DIRECT, BUT SOMEWHAT MORE EFFECTIVE APPROACH TO DEAL WITH FLAMES.
I USE THE TROLLFILTER 9000 PCIMA CARD, WITH ITS PATENTED GOONVIDIA CHIPSET™.
IT HAS HIGHLY ADVANCED FLAME DETECTION ALGORITHMS THAT AUTOMATICALLY FORWARD ANY "FLAME" EMAILS TO A CENTRAL MONITORING FACILITY WHERE TRAINED PROFESSIONALS STAND READY TO "TROUBLESHOOT" COMPLAINTS.
WHAT'S GREAT IS THAT WITH THE PREMIUM SUBSCRIPTION, YOU GET FREE "ON SITE SERVICE CALLS", WHICH I'VE FOUND TO BE PARTICULARLY EFFECTIVE.
"NYOW."
TAK TAK
TAK TAK TAK
I LOVE THIS JOB.
LETS SEE... WHO'S NEXT ON THE "TROUBLESHOOTING" LIST...

THE FOLLOWING IS A TRUE STORY...
...AND EVIDENCE THAT I SHOULD NOT GO ON VACATIONS.
YAY! WHAT A BEAUTIFUL DAY! LET'S GO FIND THAT WATERFALL!
WHY DOES THIS REMIND ME OF THE "BLAIR WITCH"?
MAMMOTH CAVE NATIONAL PARK
SER, WE'VE BEEN WALKING FOR HOURS.
ARE YOU SURE THIS IS THE RIGHT TRAIL?
OF COURSE IT IS!
MICHIGAN
UH... IT'S GETTING LATE. I DON'T THINK WE'RE GONNA MAKE IT BACK BEFORE DARK.
OH, QUIT YOUR WHINING.
A LITTLE WALK WON'T KILL YOU.
CAN YOU GET ME A CIGARETTE OUT OF MY PACK?
LOOKS LIKE YOU'RE OUT. THIS PACK IS EMPTY.
OH NO!! IT *IS* GETTING AWFUL DARK OUT! CALL 911! CALL THE PARK RANGERS!
I DON'T WANNA BE STUCK IN THE WOODS ALL NIGHT!
UH, HI. YEA, WE'RE STUCK ON THIS TRAIL...
I CAN'T SEE THE TRAIL, IT'S TOO DARK.
WE'VE GOT TO BE NEAR THAT WATERFALL BY NOW...
HEAR THAT? THAT MUST BE THE WATER-FALL!!
DRIP
DRIP
SPLISH
DRIP
SOUNDS ABOUT AS IMPRESSIVE AS A DRAIN SPOUT.
DON'T BE MEAN. WE WALKED A LONG WAY TO HEAR THIS.
WHAT'S THAT NOISE?
HELOOOO!!
PARK RANGER???
AH! THERE YOU ARE! WELL, WE'RE ABOUT A MILE FROM THE TRAIL HEAD. YOU TWO ABLE TO FOLLOW ME OUT?
I THINK SO...
LATER...
JUST ABOUT DONE WITH MY REPORT. WANNA MAKE A STATE-MEANT?
WE'RE A COUPLE OF DUMBASSES?

Failure_of_Conscience.txt

We've never really used *Megatokyo* to comment directly on current events or things going on in the world. Even when big things happen, it usually has little effect on the comic itself. This is true for most webcomics -- each one exists in its own little world and tends to resist intrusion by things from the real world.

There are times when the real world cannot be kept out. September 11, 2001 was one such day.

It was Largo who called me at the office and told me what had happened. Like many of us that day it was hard get a grasp on the enormity of it all. We joined with the many other other webcomics and websites that went "black" -- replacing the website with a black page condemning the attack and a link to the Red Cross site. After a few days, we put the site back up and produced the comic on the next page.

We all wrote a rants that summed up how we felt (you can read them in the archives on the website), but it was really hard to get back into doing comics again.

Eventually, life had to go on. Regardless of how you feel about what has happened since, it was a difficult time to live through, and I think we sometimes forget about how much it effected us all at the time.

IN AN UNPRECEDENTED TERRORIST ATTACK, TWO HIJACKED JETLINERS WERE FLOWN INTO THE TWIN TOWERS OF THE WORLD TRADE CENTER TODAY, RESULTING IN THE COLLAPSE OF THE TWO 110 STORY LANDMARKS. A THIRD HIJACKED PLANE WAS FLOWN INTO THE PENTAGON, AND A FOURTH CRASHED OUTSIDE OF PITTSBURGH. IT IS THE WORST TERRORIST ATTACK IN AMERICAN HISTORY.

INTELLIGENCE FAILURE, STRUCTURAL FAILURE...
BUT WORST OF ALL, TODAY WE HAD A FAILURE OF CONSCIENCE.
I DON'T KNOW WHAT TO SAY.
SQUEEK.

SEPTEMBER 11, 2001 - A FAILURE OF CONSCIENCE.
BUILDINGS CAN BE REBUILT, NO MATTER WHAT THE SIZE.
THE VOID IN SKY IS NOT JUST THE ABSENCE OF BUILDINGS,
BUT THE LOSS OF FAITH IN THE HUMAN CONSCIENCE.

WE HOLD OUT HOPE THAT THIS, TOO, CAN BE REBUILT.

PIRO, LARGO, SERAPHIM, DOM,
AND THE REST OF THE MT CREW.

(SIGH...)
CHRISTMAS IN A FOREIGN LAND...
ALL I'VE DONE IS CAUSE PROBLEMS FOR EVERY-ONE. I WISH I'D NEVER COME HERE.
OH? YOU REALLY THINK SO?
YOU REALLY THINK PEOPLE WOULD BE BETTER OFF IF YOU HAD NEVER MADE THIS TRIP?
ABSOLUTELY. I WISH I HAD NEVER COME.
I CAN ARRANGE THAT.
YOU CAN?
"I WISH I WAS NEVER BORN" IS TOO EXPENSIVE FOR MY BUDGET, BUT I THINK I CAN SWING THIS.
SNAP!
GIVE ME A SEC TO FIRE THIS THING UP AND...
"NETWORK IS DOWN UNTIL FURTHER NOTICE. HAPPY HOLIDAYS!"
YOU GOTTA BE KIDDING ME.
STUPID SYSTEM ADMINS. MUST BE NICE, GETTING A WHOLE WEEK OFF...

Leave it to Seraphim special! - comic analysis
CHRISTMAS IN A FOREIGN LAND...
OH? YOU REALLY THINK SO?
HEY PIRO, REMEMBER THIS COMIC?
THE CHRISTMAS ONE I NEVER FINISHED? WHAT ABOUT IT?
REMEMBER HOW PEOPLE KEPT ASKING WHY I WAS DRESSED LIKE THIS HERE....
AND THEN SUDDENLY I WAS DRESSED DIFFERENTLY...
GIVE ME A SEC TO FIRE THIS THING UP AND...
SNAP!
I GOT LOTS OF EMAIL ABOUT THIS.
ER, WELL, IT WAS OBVIOUSLY A MAGICAL GIRL TRANSFORMATION SCENE IN THIS FRAME HERE.
YOU GOTTA BE KIDDING ME.
STUPID SYSTEM ADMINS. MUST BE NICE, GETTING A WHOLE WEEK OFF...
MAYBE TO YOU IT'S OBVIOUS, BUT WHAT KIND OF MAGICAL GIRL TRANSFORMATION SEQUENCE WAS THAT? ALL YOU SEE IS MY ARM!
12.24.2001 [0208] OSE:21
EVERYONE KNOWS A REAL MAGICAL GIRL TRANSFORMATION SEQUENCE INVOLVES A SUBSTANTIAL DEGREE OF IMPLIED NUDITY.
I THINK YOU NEED TO TRY TO BE MORE AUTHENTIC. GIVE THE FANS WHAT THEY WANT TO SEE!
NO, I AM NOT DRAWING YOU NAKED.
WHAT KIND OF CONSCIENCE ARE YOU, ANYWAY?
BUT, I JUST WANT THE FANS TO BE HAPPY!
(TAKEN FROM REAL LIFE CONVERSATIONS...)

the daydream before halloween
<THAT LOOKS REALLY GOOD ON YOU, ERIKA!>
<YOU CAN TONE DOWN THE "CUTE" A LITTLE...>
PIRO! DUDE!! YOU'RE HERE!!
WHERE HAVE YOU BEEN? YOU'RE MISSIN' OUT ON FREE BOOZE!
GOMEN. I WAS BUSY COLLECTING HEADS.
HEADS? WOOO... LET ME SEE!
YEAH. I WAS OUT HUNTING DOWN RIVAL WEB COMIC ARTISTS AND COLLECTING THEIR HEADS.
SEE? THATS IAN AND MATT FROM MACHALL. NOTE THAT I'VE PACKED THEM IN SNOW.
WHO'S THE REALLY SLIMY ONE?
THAT'S POE. HE GAVE ME SOME TROUBLE.
HEY! YOU KILLED KURTZ? HE WAS A GOOD GUY!!
OOPS. SORRY. MY BAD.
HEY, WHERE'S TYCHO AND GABE?
KILLING THEM WOULD ONLY MAKE THEM STRONGER.
WEB COMIC PEOPLE HAVE BIG HEADS. HOW'D YOU GET THEM ALL TO FIT IN THAT BAG?
WITH MY SHRINK-O-MATIC WAND.
COOL-NESS! SO, DO YOU CUT 'EM OFF AND THEN SHRINK THEM, OR THE OTHER WAY AROUND?
DEPENDS ON THE DESIRED EFFECT...
<UHM... HE DOESN'T REALLY HAVE HEADS IN THAT BAG, DOES HE?>
<DUNNO. HIS CONSCIENCE HAS BEEN BUSY WITH MIDTERMS LATELY.>

TODAY ON "LARGO" WE HAVE SOME VERY SPECIAL GUESTS FROM *BIOWARE*, TRENT OSTER AND BRAD GRIER! LET'S HAVE A BIG ROUND OF APPLAUSE FOR OUR GUESTS!
SO, WHAT'S IT LIKE MAKING GAMES ALL DAY?
WE MAKE GAMES?
I THOUGHT WE WERE A DEFENSE CONTRACTOR FOR THE CANADIAN SPACE DEFENSE FORCE?
GAH! SHHHHH!
HAHAHA!! DON'T PAY ANY ATTENTION TO HIM! OF COURSE WE MAKE GAMES! GOOD ONES TOO!
WHAT ABOUT THE CANADA PLAN FOR GLOBAL DOMINATION?
AHAHAH!!! WE MAKE EXCELLENT GAMES, LIKE "BALDUR'S GATE"! AND "NEVER-WINTER NIGHTS"!
I THOUGHT "NEVER-WINTER NIGHTS" WAS THE CODENAME FOR THAT MIND CONTROL APPLICATION THAT WE...
DAMN. THERE GOES THAT PLAN.
WELL, THERE'S ALWAYS "SHATTERED STEEL 2."
WAY TO GO, BOSS.
WOAH THERE BRAD! LET'S PUT THAT CHAIR DOWN! SECURITY! DOM! ED!!

while reports of our death
were premature, it might
have been easier than battling the...

attack of the hosting hobgoblins

HI FOLKS, WE'RE BACK.

WE APOLOGIZE FOR THE DOWNTIME, BUT THINGS SHOULD BE SETTLING DOWN TO NORMAL FAIRLY SOON. PARDON OUR DUST AS WE GET SITUATED INTO OUR NEW HOME.

PIRO

HEY DUDE, WHAT'S WITH THE CLEAN SUIT? WORRIED ABOUT DUST?
YOU'RE FIXING THE SERVER. NAKED. DO I REALLY HAVE TO EXPLAIN?
I SEE THAT THE OLD RAID CONTROLLER GOT "THE SCREW-DRIVER."
IT WAS NOT L33T. IT DESERVED DE4TH.
WENDY'S
mt LABS

early in 2002 we had to find new hosting for the website, and we were offline for a few weeks.

HI FOLKS,
AS YOU MAY ALREADY KNOW, SERAPHIM AND I ARE MOVING OVER THE NEXT FEW WEEKS.
IN AN EFFORT TO MAINTAIN WHAT LITTLE SANITY I HAVE LEFT, EVERY SO OFTEN I'M GOING TO COP OUT AND DO "LITE" COMICS, LIKE THIS ONE.
A "LITE" COMIC IS A COMIC THAT DOESN'T TAKE 8 HOURS TO MAKE.

THAT DOESN'T MEAN THAT A "LITE" COMIC CAN'T BE FUNNY, IT JUST MEANS THAT I DON'T HAVE TO DO SO MANY DRAWINGS.
I STILL INTEND TO DO AT LEAST TWO "NORMAL" COMICS EACH WEEK WHILE WE ARE IN THE MIDDLE OF OUR MOVE.
OFFICIAL WINGED BACKPACK FROM *KANON*

i've moved 3 times since megatokyo started. not once was i ahead enough that i didn't have to skip comics.

OH, AND I DON'T KNOW WHO STARTED THE VICIOUS RUMOR THAT I'VE BEEN SPENDING ALL MY TIME WATCHING THE NEW *KANON* ANIME OVER AND OVER AGAIN...
UGUUU~~
IT'S JUST NOT TRUE! REALLY! I'VE BEEN WORKING VERY HARD, ORGANIZING AND PACKING MY STUFF...

I DON'T CONSIDER ARCHIVING YOUR ANIME FILES ONTO CDROMS "PACKING."
NOW GET YOUR LAZY BUTT OVER HERE AND HELP ME PACK UP THE KITCHEN.

AHHH....
NEVERWINTER NIGHTS.
YOU HAVE SUCKED MY SOUL DRY, YOU HAVE INSPIRED CHANGES IN MY PERSONAL HYGIENE.
TRULY, THE BEST GAME EVER.
HOW DID I EVER LIVE WITHOUT YOU?

(SIGH)
EVEN THE BOX IS BEAUTIFUL.

HMMMMMMMMMMMMMM....

DUDE, HERE FEEL THE BOX. IT'S SO SMOOTH.
THE LAST TIME YOU HANDED ME A BOX IT WAS ALL STICKY. GET AWAY FROM ME.

August 14th, 2002
MEGATOKYO IS OFFICIALLY TWO YEARS OLD TODAY.
YAY.
FIRST, I'D LIKE TO APOLOGIZE FOR ALL THE DELAYS, DEAD PIRO ART DAYS, SHIRT GUY DOM DAYS, DOM, GUEST STRIP DAYS, MISSED STRIPS, SUB-STANDARD STRIPS LACK OF RANTS, LACK OF COHESIVE STORY, SLOW PACE, POOR DRAWING QUALITY, LACK OF HUMOR AND OVERALL SUCKAGE THAT HAS PLAGUED THIS SAD EXCUSE FOR A "WEBCOMIC" FOR THE PAST TWO YEARS...
YOU DONE?
UHM, WELL, NOT REALLY, I STILL...
I THINK YOU'RE DONE.
OK.
THERE ARE A LOT OF PEOPLE I NEED TO THANK FOR ALL THEIR HARD WORK AND SUPPORT. THERE ISN'T ENOUGH ROOM HERE TO DO IT, BUT THERE SHOULD BE IN MY RANT COLUMN.
I THINK.
FINALLY, FOR THOSE OF YOU OUT THERE WHO I'VE HAD... "ISSUES" WITH...
DOM AND ED WILL BE DROPPING BY TO MAKE SURE THAT ALL "ISSUES" ARE "TAKEN CARE OF".
THERE ARE THE SELECT FEW THAT I WILL DEAL WITH PER-SONALLY, RIGHT?
YEP, OF COURSE. YOU ALWAYS GET FIRST PICK.
GOOD.

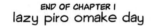

END OF CHAPTER 1

lazy piro omake day

WELL, I WAS ORIGINALLY GOING TO DO A MORE COMPLICATED "OMAKE" ("EXTRA, BONUS" -MANY ANIME HAVE SHORT LITTLE SKITS AT THE END OF THE TAPE - USUALLY SHORT, USUALLY GOOFY) AND IN FACT, THIS IS KIND OF AN "OMAKE" WEEK. WE'VE BEEN WORKING ON GETTING CHAPTER 2 PUT TOGETHER, AS WELL AS ISSUES WITH THE WEBSITE, CHARACTER AND STORY INFORMATION, ETC, ETC. IT'S ALL A LOT OF WORK, AND I GOTTA DO IT SOMETIME. I SORTA DIDN'T LEAVE ENOUGH "EXTRA" TONIGHT TO FINISH THIS ONE - OH WELL. PLEASE ACCEPT MY APOLOGIES, AND A MORE "CONDENSED" VERSION OF THE PLANNED OMAKE. ^^;;

PIRO

this filler comic had more to do with wanting to play with my new laptop than anything else.

CHAPTER 2 OFFICIAL
can't find dom filler

WITH APOLOGIES TO
BERKE BREATHED (*BLOOM COUNTY*)

Dead_Piro_Art_Days.txt

Like I mentioned earlier, there are times when I just can't finish a comic and end up putting up some sort of filler. Most of the time these are in the form of Dead Piro Days.

A Dead Piro Day is pretty much just that -- I feel pretty dead and don't feel like or have time to do a normal comic, so i do a single drawing instead.

A typical MT comic takes about eight hours of work, but a Dead Piro Day usually requires no more than an hour or so of random free sketching. Sometimes doing a comic can be stressful -- doing all the drawings, scanning them, setting things up in Illustrator, modifying the dialogue, making sure things fit with previous comics … Working on a single more random drawing can be relaxing and almost therapeutic in comparison. :)

The following pages contain most of the Dead Piro Days that appeared in Chapter 1 and Chapter 2. Most of the comments on them appear as they do online. I've added new comments to some of them on little sticky notes.

In Chapter 2 you may have noticed some drawings that appear randomly featuring Pirogoeth and Largo in what appears to be some sort of fantasy game setting. This is an example how some Dead Piro Art Days ended up threading their way into the story. This sequence eventually ended up becoming part of Miho's waking dream.

Dead Piro Art Days are an important part of *Megatokyo*, often having some point, clue, or odd comment about the story. Readers seem to like them - as long as I don't miss TOO many story comics.

discarded frames

some weeks you just can't win, this is one of them. the real killer this week has been discarded frames - drawings that just don't work the way i wanted them to. this is one such frame. The elusive next comic is almost done, i just need to spend some time working on it tomorrow night. Should be ready for sunday. thank you for your patience, sorry that this week is just a total write-off.

-piro-

i draw each frame separately, usually two per 8.5x11 sheet. i print templates like this one to draw on.

this is a raw sketch. i haven't cleaned up any of the smudges or stray lines.

monday - tuesday - wednesday - thursday - friday

sheet episode chap number

HI EVERYONE. AS YOU MAY HAVE READ, SERAPHIM AND I WILL BE GOING AWAY FOR A ONE WEEK VACATION NEXT MONTH.

I SOMEHOW DOUBT I WILL HAVE 3 STRIPS READY TO GO BEFORE I LEAVE.

SO WE CAME UP WITH THIS SILLY CONTEST TO HELP US FILL IN THE VOID...

we had over 50 submissions f this. it would h been easier to 3 comics than to judge them

people still bug me to make plushies like these.

The Vacationing Piro Guest Strip Contest

THE CONTEST IS SIMPLE. COME UP WITH YOUR OWN MEGATOKYO STRIP AND SEND US A LINK TO THE FINISHED COMIC. PLEASE DON'T EMAIL THE FILE UNLESS YOU HAVE NO OTHER WAY OF GETTING IT TO US. ALL STRIPS SHOULD BE EXACTLY 650 PIXLES WIDE, AND CAN BE ANYWHERE FROM 650 TO 975 PIXLES TALL. GIF OR JPG FILES ARE ACCEPTABLE. YES, THEY CAN BE IN COLOR. STRIPS WILL BE JUDGED ON OVERALL QUALITY - NOT JUST ART, NOT JUST THE GAG. KEEP IT CLEAN - PG-13 PLEASE.

FOR MORE INFORMATION, GO TO

contest in July 2

DEADLINE IS **FRIDAY JULY 6, 10:00 PM EDT** (THAT'S ONE WEEK FROM TODAY)

WE WILL PICK FIVE STRIPS WE THINK ARE THE MOST ENTERTAINING AND POST ONE PER DAY FOR THE WEEK OF JULY 9 THRU 13, WITH THE BEST STRIP GOING UP ON FRIDAY. AND THE WINNING STRIP EVEN GET'S A PRIZE!

YA YA, I KNOW - NO REAL MT STRIPS FOR A **WEEK!** BUMMER. HEY, IT COULD BE WORSE. I COULD LET DOM DO A WEEK'S WORTH OF SHIRT GUY DOM STRIPS - OR WOULD THAT BE CONSIDERED 'FAN ABUSE'? ^_^

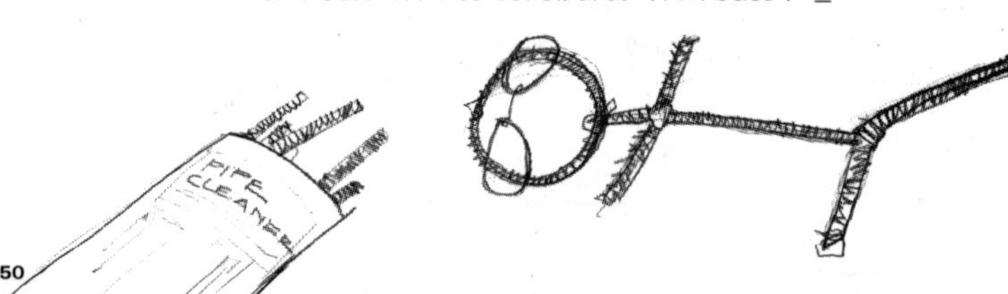

break time

DEAD PIRO DAY, REALLY. I'M FEELING LAZY, SO I JUST SAT DOWN AND SCRIBBLED THIS OUT INSTEAD. LIKE SERAPHIM'S NEW HAIRSTYLE? ITS PRETTY CUTE. OH YA, SHE'S REALLY GOT THOSE PANTS, TOO.

piro art day - 002

FIRST OFF, SORRY ABOUT MISSING FRIDAY'S COMIC - SINCE THIS IS THE ONLY WEEKEND I HAVE TO PREPARE FOR OTAKON, I DECIDED TO USE IT THAT WAY. ^_^ HERE IS A LITTLE TEASER SHOWING THE SECOND FULL COLOR IMAGE THAT WE'RE PREPARING FOR OTAKON - A IMAGE FROM PIRO'S DATING-SIM WORLD, SO TO SPEAK...

OH, AND IF YOU DIDN'T KNOW, TRYING TO DESIGN SCHOOL-GIRL UNIFORMS IS NOT AS EASY AS IT LOOKS... ^^;;

- PIRO, SUNDAY AFTERNOON

HISTORY LESSON: "WARMTH" WAS THE STORY I WAS WORKING ON BEFORE *MEGATOKYO* STARTED, ONE I HOPE TO GET BACK TO SOMEDAY. I HAVEN'T DRAWN THE "WARMTH" CHARACTERS IN AGES. IT WAS FUN DRAWING SAEKO AND TOM AGAIN. REMEMBER, *MEGATOKYO* WAS NEVER SUPPOSED TO HAPPEN – THIS WAS:

warmth
saeko tobari
tom blackenmoor
just a small, unimportant story around some rather unimportant events in the city of Sendai, Japan.
it probably wouldn't have happened in tokyo.
for one thing, it snows more in Sendai...
people have been bugging me to work on "warmth" since i posted this. i've been working on it ever since.

END OF CHAPTER 1
lazy piro omake # 3

this is a horrible drawing of Kimiko, but some people seemed to like it. designing uber cute outfits isn't easy.

piro's sketchbook - peek #1

NOTE: COMMENTS BY SONODA YUKI

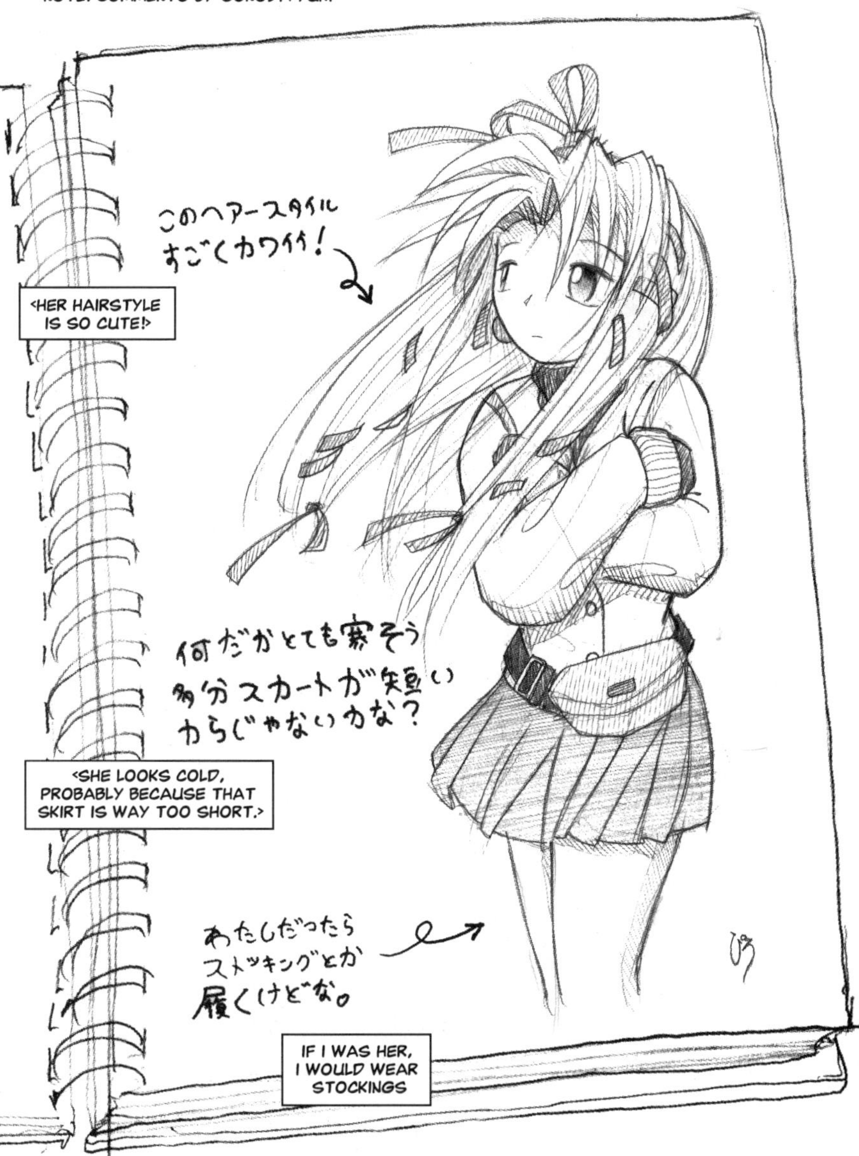

このヘアースタイル
すごくカワイイ!
<HER HAIRSTYLE IS SO CUTE!>
何だかとても寒そう
多分スカートが短い
からじゃないかな?
<SHE LOOKS COLD, PROBABLY BECAUSE THAT SKIRT IS WAY TOO SHORT.>
わたしだったら
ストッキングとか
履くけどな。
IF I WAS HER, I WOULD WEAR STOCKINGS

KITTIE
Nanasawa & Piro
"waiting for the show"
(note, this sketch has not been touched up or cleaned up at all. this is what a raw scan looks like.)
the original drawing will be on display this weekend at Otakon2002, and will be auctioned off to support the MT New Server fund.
yes, those are kitty ears on her hoodie, and yes, piro's cap flops into sad kitty ears...
the sale of this drawing helped me buy a new server for megatokyo. the old server was on it's last legs.

field cleaning

DEAD PIRO WEEK - 1 OF 4

I SORT OF NEED TO TAKE A BREAK FROM MEGATOKYO FOR ABOUT A WEEK TO GET MY BEARINGS. I HAD TO BE REALISTIC ABOUT THINGS THIS WEEK, AND THAT'S WHY I AM LISTING THE NEXT FEW DAYS AS A "BREAK" SO I CAN GET SOME OTHER THINGS TAKEN CARE OF.

i needed a break so i did a series of DPD drawings. freesketching can be therapeutic. :)

3x3eyes/bannoubunkaneckmusume

DEAD PIRO WEEK - DAY 2 OF 4

- A TRIBUTE TO YUZO TAKADA -

YUZO TAKADA, THE MAN BEHIND "3X3 EYES", "ALL PURPOSE CULTURAL CAT GIRL NUKU NUKU", "BLUE SEED", AND "EVERY DAY IS SUNDAY" HAS BEEN A PRETTY BIG INFLUENCE ON ME, BOTH IN TERMS OF STORYTELLING AND IN HIS ART. I'VE ALWAYS LOVED THE STORY BETWEEN PAI AND YAKUMO, MUCH OF THE 3X3 EYES MANGA I HAVE I COLLECTED WHILE TRAVELING IN JAPAN. THE WAY I SHADE EYES I CAN TRACE BACK TO HIS WORK.

HERE WE HAVE KIMIKO AS "PAI" (YES, THAT IS A 3RD EYE) PIRO AS "YAKUMO" (ER, IT DOESN'T WORK VERY WELL... PIRO IS WAY TOO DORKY TO BE YAKUMO) AND PING AS NUKU NUKU (VERY APPROPRIATE, SINCE NUKU NUKU IS ONE OF THE INFLUENCES ON PING'S DESIGN.)

DOUMO ARIGATOU, TAKADA-SENSEI.

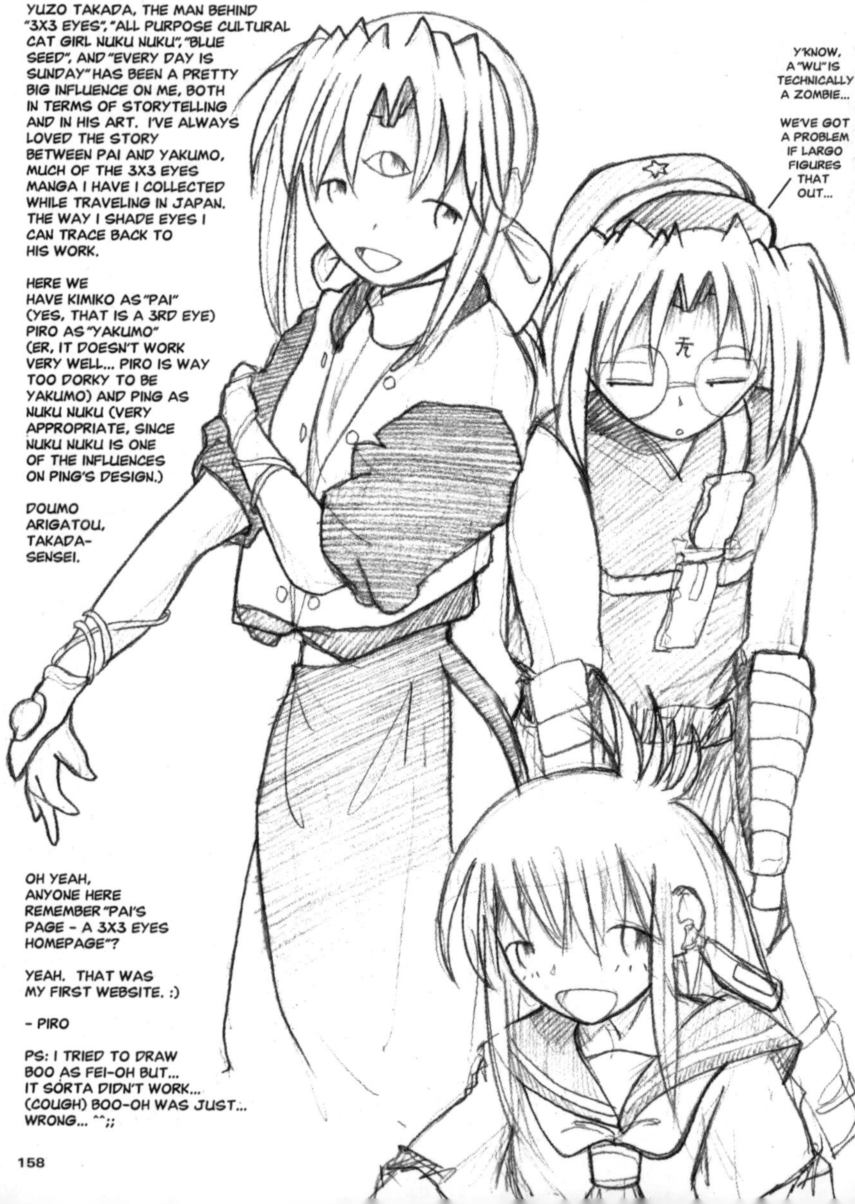

Y'KNOW, A "WU" IS TECHNICALLY A ZOMBIE...
WE'VE GOT A PROBLEM IF LARGO FIGURES THAT OUT...

OH YEAH, ANYONE HERE REMEMBER "PAI'S PAGE - A 3X3 EYES HOMEPAGE"?

YEAH. THAT WAS MY FIRST WEBSITE. :)

- PIRO

PS: I TRIED TO DRAW BOO AS FEI-OH BUT... IT SORTA DIDN'T WORK... (COUGH) BOO-OH WAS JUST... WRONG... ^^;;

dance of the evils
ダンス・オブ・ザ・イーヴルズ
monday night 9:00pm
6月10日(月)、21:00
cave of evil
ケイヴ・オヴ・イーヴル
場所:原宿
(03) 3845-228x
sorvse of evil for harajuku . by dj pokki

mywingsareonlysmallwings

DEAD PIRO WEEK - DAY 4 OF 4

AND THAT'S THAT. THIS DRAWING IS NO WHERE NEAR AS NICE AS I HAD INTENDED (IN FACT, I ALMOST CRUMPLED IT UP) BUT I GUESS IT'S STILL BETTER THAN THE FIRST DPD IN THIS SERIES.

nodatacanfilltheemptyspaces
DEAD PIRO WEEK - DAY 5 OF 4
UGH, JUST ONE MORE. I OVERDID IT OVER THE WEEKEND, FELL ASLEEP AT MY DESK MONAY NIGHT AT 10PM, AND CONSEQUENTLY DIDN'T HAVE ENOUGH TIME TO FINISH THE SCRIPT AND GET THE COMIC DONE. GOMEN.
PING IS SHOWN HERE WITH HER HAIR DOWN, NOTE THAT IT IS QUITE LONG.
HER LEFT EARBLADE CONTAINS ALL HER BASIC CONTROLS. THE STATUS SCREEN IS DESIGNED TO BE EASY TO READ WHEN TALKING TO HER.
HER LEFT EARBLADE ALSO HAS VIDEO OUT CONNECTIONS AS WELL AS 2 USB PORTS TO CONNECT INPUT DEVICES, SUCH AS A KEYBOARD.
SONY
LABS
HER RIGHT EARBLADE IS FOR I/O AND POWER CONNECTIONS. RIGHT NOW, SHE IS USING A FIREWIRE AND A FAST ETHERNET CONNECTION. SEGMENTS OF HER PROCESSOR CORE ARE ISOLATED FROM EACH OTHER AND REQUIRE SEPERATE HARDWIRE CONNECTIONS
PING DOES NOT HAVE A WI-FI WIRELESS NIC - IT IS AN OPTION THAT WILL BE AVAILIBLE IN PRODUCTION MODELS

3vilhasmanyguises

sight
サイト
this is an early drawing of Kotone, the character that Kimiko is auditioning to play in the game "Sight."
the "Girl of nothing but grays" has evolved over time, as you can see in the next few drawings.
kotone
ことね
lockart
cubesoft

agirlofnothingbutgreys..

神無月琴音
kannazuki kotone

Megatokyo_Gameworlds.txt

While what we do in our real lives will always be important, what we do in our online lives is becoming increasingly a part of what makes us who we are. Many of us spend a lot of time playing games and living in virtual worlds. Yes, we all know they are games, but it is silly to dismiss them as unimportant. These activities are something we are very proud of and work very hard to maintain.

Since games are such an important part of Piro and Largo's life, it's only natural that these experiences, both past and present, will have some bearing on the story. Largo is pretty much always Largo -- his online persona is not very different from the way he is in real life. Piro is quite different -- he plays female characters (Piroko in FPS games, Pirogoeth or Pirokiko in online RPG games, etc) and his approach to things online is far more determined than the way he approaches things in real life.

One game that they used to play in *Megatokyo* is an online Massively Multiplayer Online Roll Playing Game (MMORPG) called Endgames. What happened in Endgames is important to the *Megatokyo* story, and I have done a variety of drawings to help develop the concept.

For extra material in this book, I finished a short story that I started back when i first developed the Endgames concept. This short story features a small snippet of the adventures of Pirogoeth and Largo in the game, as the game characters might see it. More about this game and its bearing on the Megatokyo story will become clear over time :P

this is piroko and largo from one of their "quakeworld" mods. This drawing later became a full color poster.
HEY, I THOUGHT THIS WAS SUPPOSED TO BE A CAPTURE THE B33R MOD?
HUSH.

WOOT! THAT KICKED A55! I NEED A BEER! I MEAN, AN AL3!

I AGREE. KILLING MAKES ME THIRSTY.

THERE'S AN INN OVER HERE. I THINK I COULD USE AN ALE OR TWO MYSELF.

ZOUNDS! WRONG INN!!

OK, I'M NOT THIRSTY ANYMORE.

NOT YOU THREE AGAIN.

BUT WAIT, GUYS, THEY HAVE MAGIC BEER HERE!

AM I THE ONLY ONE WHO'S REALLY DISTURBED SEEING PIROGOETH IN A BARMAID'S DRESS?

I'M GOING TO GOUGE OUT MY EYES. GIVE ME ONE OF THOSE ARROWS.

endgamestanding

see the website for
the full color version
of this. note the
original concept had
largo looming in the
background, but i
wasn't happy with it.

Endgames: Presence

A *Megatokyo* Gameworlds short story by Fred Gallagher

"Aye, This be the most sad excuse for ale I've yet to encounter!"

The innkeeper looked up from his task to see a tall, burly man with weather-stained leathers and a huge shock of red hair point an accusing mug at him. He was swaying from side to side and eyed him with an expression of religious disbelief and abhorrence.

"You, sir, should be strung up from the nearest tree, and then dunked in a vat of your own vile ale which assuredly will dissolve the very flesh from your bones! The sale, nay, even the free gift of such a putrid brew is an affront to the gods of Ale themselves!!"

"Ya wants another?"

"That I do."

"It would be appreciated if you were to drown yourself in your next pint, for I am sick of your bellowing," commented the man's companion, a small, slight woman sitting with her back to the wall, giving her partner a look that would set the fear of the more violent gods into most men.

He lifted his newly filled mug and glanced at her. "Pirogoeth, you shame me. You have yet to finish your first cup of this bilge," He turned to her with a smug grin, set a solidly shod foot on the bench where she was sitting and leaned heavily towards her. "It pains me to have a companion who knoweth not the joy of the enchanted brews. It is true magic, I say, true to the earth, true to the soul! Your witchcraft is but a sham, a trick, a hollow gesture compared to the mystic delights of even this bilious brew." He gripped the mug warmly with both hands and leaned closer, "It is a magic that overcomes the horror of its reality, the vileness of its bitterness, the repugnance of its putridity and transports you to a plane of utter rapture where true bliss is found!"

She wrinkled her nose and recoiled from his tirade, or more precisely, his breath. "For the sake of the seven goddesses, Largo, do not breathe on me. If magic it is, it's of the offensive sort."

Largo leaned back and laughed heartily. With a flourish, he emptied the mug, wiped his mouth on his sleeve, and set off to needle the innkeeper for more.

Pirogoeth gave him a withering look. In the many months they had been traveling together her urge to reduce him to a smoldering pile of black cinders had not diminished with time. Their pairing was the result of an odd twist of fate and circumstance had given her little say in her choice of traveling companions. At least his massive size and overbearing presence made traveling safer. She was as dangerous if not more so than he was, but the average brigand tended to judge her easy prey and proving the error of this was tiring and messy.

Largo returned with yet another full mug and planted himself solidly on the bench next to her with a loud creak. He breathed deeply, brought the mug to his lips, and drained the cup with a long, noisy draft.

Averting her eyes from his rather brutish consumption of ale she looked at her own mug, of which she had barely consumed half of its contents. Even this small amount of drink was having an effect on her. She felt a pleasant, calming warmth in her cheeks. The smoky haze of the common room, the flickering candle light, the dancing shadows from the fire, and the noisy drone of conversation....

Largo belched loudly and triumphantly planted the empty mug on the rough table with a heavy bang. She wondered if it was his large body mass or relative lack of brain matter that allowed him to drink so many mugs of the potent brew. She quietly wished he would go away.

"Ahhh, much better," he said, leaning against the wall making himself comfortable. He turned his head and cocked an eye at her. "You seem to be in a wondrous mood, as usual."

She didn't turn her head to look at him. "My mood is not now, nor is it ever, any of your business."

He chuckled. "Yer a rotten excuse for a woman," he proclaimed, leaning forward to look her up and down with a critical eye. "Aye, pathetic. Ya don't even have the womanly parts. More like a little boy with pigtails than a woman. You might at least smile once in a while, like a proper woman. Finish the cup, it will do you wonders."

For a brief moment, she recalled the words to that spell. It was a good spell, one that struck fear into the hearts of any that witnessed it. Rending, shredding, flaying, burning, all wrapped up into one nasty, horrible experience for the unfortunate victim. She wondered how often Largo toyed with death this way.

"I'd prefer to keep this evening's meal where it is, and where it will do me some good. If you choose to wash out your innards with drink, that is your affair." Despite the bitterness of the ale, it had a mellowing effect. Her lack of desire to move was probably the only thing between Largo and the evisceration spell of which she was so fond.

He spit noisily into a corner and leaned back, cradling his arms behind his head. "Pah, I've hardly drunk enough to satisfy my thirst, never mind enough to be causin' me to pitch the evening meal. Besides," he said with a grunt, "I do not like it here. We are strangers, and this is a strange town. We must be careful. Our presence is not...welcome."

She looked around at the decrepit old room and its shabby occupants. "I would assume that travelers are not that unusual here. This is an old inn and the highway that runs through the town is part of the ancient trade route between Kaieskallen and Fougoureth. Even people like myself who are not travelers are familiar with it."

"Aye, but that be not the way things are in these dark times. Traders and caravans travel far south to avoid the edges of these forests, and did so even before our own lands fell silent. 'Tis safer to brave the harsh mountain passes of the edgelands than the gloomy highways of this forest. If you look about, there are naught but locals here. More men than usual are avoiding you, and even excessive drinking is doing little to lighten their mood. I do not like it here. There is evil afoot."

Pirogoeth had learned over time that Largo's seemingly paranoid and over-reactionary observations were not to be dismissed without investigation. Often he would point towards a wood and say "those trees are evil!" and it was always true that at least one actually was. Ignoring this observation once led to her suffering many bruises from a hail of apples hurled at her by just such a tree.

There was little here that seemed threatening. The inn was a small, ancient establishment nestled in a grove of trees in the middle of town. It was not a large town, and seemed plain and ordinary enough when they had arrived earlier that evening. Most of the people in the common room seemed to be locals, dressed in the dull, mud-worn leathers and coarse fabrics common to these lands. There was a quiet din of discussion, but most of the room's occupants seemed to be focused on reducing themselves into unconsciousness as soon as possible.

Largo was much taller than all the other men in the room, and far broader. He wore his mail and serviceable yet ornate armor as if it weighed little more than a linen shirt. She wondered if any of them had ever seen a Reaht legionnaire before. His massive, looming presence and brash manner fairly obviously made the locals uncomfortable.

She supposed that she, too, was an exotic presence. Local women did not wear much in the way of armor or girt themselves with weapons. Even simple men could sense the magical capacity of another, and she was sure that her skills in Thaumaturgy would be considered dangerous and unwelcome. Her pale complexion and straw colored hair was also uncommon this far north. Everything about her was out of place here.

She touched the mark on her face. It was a stain, not a scar. A stain left by an enemy's blood. Blood that had soaked her hands and stained her face as she wiped away tears in the cold, shadowy mist...

It was unlikely that they would be mistaken for simple traders. She was not surprised people were avoiding them.

"I sense little danger here, except perhaps the presence of yet undiscovered diseases caught from excessive exposure to dirt." She lifted the mug to her lips and took a small sip. She grimaced, and took another, feeling it go straight to her face. If Largo was to make any comment on the color of her cheeks she would rend him into a simmering puddle of fat and charred bone and feel no guilt.

She glanced at him and saw that he wasn't looking at her. He had stiffened, his entire being tightening like a bowstring as his attention focused on a looming threat somewhere that only he could feel. As was often the case, the brooding evil he sensed was probably entirely in his head, a by-product of days of boring travel without incident. She raised an eyebrow and gave him a flat look.

"We are being watched," he said, indicating a dim corner to the far side of the room, away from the fireplace. Several figures were seated there, but all seemed more interested in the pewter mugs before them than anything else in the room.

Largo rose to his feet with a jittery clink of mail and the hushed creak of leather. He towered above her, glaring intently at the men seated quietly in the offensive corner. She looked up at him, knowing what was about to transpire. "Largo, I would for one night like to sleep in a real bed and not on the cold soggy ground. If you—"

"Shhh," he snapped, with a backward motion of his hand. "I must face this threat. I will not allow this evil to mock me."

Like a looming thunderstorm, he strode across the room towards the unsuspecting drinkers. Pirogoeth shot his departing back an irritated glare and thought for a brief moment of countering his advance. She decided not to. If he felt the need to start a fight in the common room and get himself tossed out into the cold, wet, muddy night, then he could sleep in a soggy ditch by himself. She was not going to let him ruin her chances of sleep in a soft bed and perhaps even the chance of a bath. She wondered if the inn could provide her with one. Traveling with Largo made her feel the need for one on an almost daily basis.

She watched as Largo sat himself squarely in the middle of the group, startling the brooding drinkers. She couldn't hear what was being said, but was relieved to see that he appeared to be attempting the warm, friendly approach first rather than his usual overt aggression. In spite of his easy, overly friendly manner, she did notice that he had unsnapped the holding straps on the massive broadsword sheathed across his back. Heads would probably roll and blood would probably spill, but not for a while yet.

He gave a thunderous call for more ale and laughed heartily, throwing his arm around the shoulder of a fellow drinker. The man seemed to smile nervously and was not sure what to make of the man almost twice his size. The surly innkeeper brought more mugs, and soon everyone at the table was drinking freely. Maybe she would get lucky and he would drink himself into oblivion with his newfound drinking partners. Maybe she could slip away quietly and inquire about that bath.

She turned her attention to her own mug. The drink was not really as bad as Largo made it

sound. There was the strong taste of some bitter fruit in the brew that was almost palatable. She took another long sip, sat back against the wall and closed her eyes.

There was no sense of presence in the room. No watchful, brooding evil. No unsettling sense of dread. Often, Largo's hair-trigger observations about harmful things around them had helped her tune in on things she had trouble sensing or things that were well hidden. She focused on the tensions that might be in the air, or the wobble in the fabric of reality that can form around unnatural threats, but there was nothing. It was a simple common room filled with simple locals comforting themselves after a long, normal, work-filled day. They drank and brooded away the evening with quiet discussions about unseen darkness at the edges of their world.

There was nothing. She huddled herself more firmly against the wall and wrapped her cloak closer about her. Shadows from the fire danced on the far wall, and she watched them with pale, olive-colored eyes.

Burning, falling, smoldering, ash, mist, nothingness. Memories that were always on the edge of her thoughts. Her mind played through them, like an old story that no longer held the power to bring forth tears, but still haunted the edges of her consciousness....

A city besieged. Its people—her people—battling conquering forces from the south. Suddenly, a new threat came in with the wind from the darkening sea to the east. Sickly green sails of uncountable dark ships. Death came in great waves even before the ships reached the shore. Destruction was somehow inevitable, it flowed through the city, taking its life and extinguishing it. The very fabric of the world seemed to waver, fold, and take everything away. Shadowy armies of uncountable foes surged thru the city. Death came violently, quietly. Buildings collapsed and fell into ashen ruin. Mists crawled up the cliffs and swallowed her city with a sigh. Even the Reahthan besiegers, the conquering forces from the south, were not safe from the onslaught. They too were caught up and dissolved away into the mists that caused the eastern coastal realm of Kuith to exist no more.

She had felt a presence that day, something just beyond the edge of sight and beyond the edge of perception. Something watching, vast and omnipresent that could overwhelm her very being with its mere existence.

The only slightly more solid dark figures that came ashore to claim the remains of her realm seemed to spare her only so she could witness its death. Cold shock and dread made her a quiet captive, but in the end they had underestimated her. She sensed the confusion and anger of the presence as she stood amid the slain bodies of its captains. It grew cold, distant, seemed to fade, and then she was alone. As she left the faded shell of her lands behind, they slowly faded away and were no more. She knew that she could not take even a single step back, for there wasn't anything there anymore.

And now, here she sat, huddled in a coarse cloak watching dancing shadows on the smoke-stained walls of an inn far from the vanished remains of her lands. She accompanied the very captain that had led the siege against her city. Much like herself, he had lost his legions and his men, and later found that he too had lost his country. They were adrift in the world with nothing to return to because their lands didn't exist anymore.

Even the most solid things in her life had melted away and vanished, but the shadowy presence she could not see, feel, or sense clearly had become the only thing that she knew was real. It haunted her dreams, plagued her memories, and hovered at the edges of her reality as if her waking life could be snatched away at any moment. Largo, too, could sense this "presence." Perhaps the fact that he could sense it yet in no way seize or confront it had driven him mad. Maybe his crazy and unpredictable nature was his way of defying it.

For some reason, it seemed to be their fate to pursue this presence and its malevolent purpose. Sometimes it seemed as if they were following it in some attempt to exact revenge and rid the world of its destructive grip. Other times it was as if they were fleeing from it, trying to find some safe corner of the world where it could not haunt them any further.

Tonight, she was too tired and too solemn to care. She was grateful for the simple feel of a warm cloak, the dancing shadows of a warm fire, the lingering weight of a simple meal, and the bitter, fruity taste of a cup of the local ale. There was no presence plaguing her reality tonight, and for that she was grateful.

Just because you cannot sense it, does not mean that it is not here.

Pirogoeth's reality snapped back into place with a brutal suddenness. Her eyes came into sharp focus as she sat up perfectly straight, quivering with solid, abrupt tension. She had slowly been falling into a sleepy daze, drifting away with the effects of the ale and her own quiet thoughts, but that last thought was not hers. She had felt it, but it was from somewhere outside of her.

She slowly looked about the room. Nothing had changed. Locals muttered over pots of ale and the smoky fire danced in its hearth. Largo was laughing heartily, slapping a smaller man on the back as they shared some ridiculous tale made funnier by the brew. Several rounds of ale had improved the spirits of his companions as they joined in the laughter. The innkeeper was collecting empty mugs from a table. There was a small flare and pop from the fire.

She stood, slowly, her leathers creaking softly as she pushed the bench back with a scrape. There was a quiet chink of her belt as it settled across her hips, and a rasp as the edges of shoulder plates moved over each other. She stared at the wall with the dancing shadows.

"Largo," she said as the hair on the back of her neck stood on edge.

There was a cold, deep tonal rasp as Largo drew his broadsword from its sheath. The suddenness of this motion startled everyone in the room, which grew suddenly quiet. The men he had been drinking with shrank away from the sudden change that had come over the foreigner.

Something was there. She could not see it, nor could she perceive it with her senses, but she *knew* it was there. Everything before this had been merely echoes, weak memories of an overwhelming presence that was a threat to her very being. This was different. This was no echo. This was no distant memory. It was here.

"Aye, Pirogoeth! What sense ye?" Largo bellowed as he stood away from the table, broadsword firmly covering all before him. His eyes covered the entire room as he backed towards where Pirogoeth stood. Tall, grim, solid, there was no sign of excessive drinking in his stance.

The innkeeper yelled out for him to put his weapon away, but Largo ignored him. There was an angry mutter from the crowd. All were standing now, eyeing darkly the grim man and the strange woman who suddenly seemed dangerous and threatening

She glared at the wall, at the place where she knew there was a gap. Not a gap in the wall, but a gap in the air, a gap in the space before the wall. Something was standing there. It was bigger than the room, dwarfing everything about it. It filled the space, yet somehow it wasn't there. It was chuckling to itself. It was laughing at her, amused with her efforts to see it.

She felt Largo's massive presence come up to where she stood, still as stone. "It seems the evil cannot handle its ale," he said, watching the room about them. "The lad in the corner was a weak point. After a few pints, he fell

apart. These folk are possessed. It is a dead town. The game is upon us."

Suddenly, the presence was gone. No, not gone—moved, so she could no longer focus on it. She looked about her. The room was silent. The townsfolk stood around them, blocking the both ends of the room. The crackling of the fire was the only sound.

Something had changed. Blank, expressionless faces looked toward them, focused on nothing. A huge, squat, bearded man stumbled forward a step, his eyes and face blank, his arms lifted before him. Another followed. Soon, the mass of them was slowly, quietly, inexorably, creeping toward them from both sides of the room.

"It seems that these good townsfolk feel we have outstayed our welcome," said Largo, changing the grip on his sword. He swung the massive blade in a huge arc, crushing the very air itself as he steadied it before him in an invincible and threatening stance.

Pirogoeth knew Largo was grinning from ear to ear, even though she could not see his face. They were back to back as the mindless crowd slowly stumbled towards them. She drew her own sword, much smaller in stature than Largos. Pitted, unadorned, it was a randomly abandoned blade that she had haphazardly picked up in a daze after her life had come crashing down around her. It was a blade that held no meaning, no importance. She drew no comfort from it. These were not her kind of battles.

"I believe the exit from this establishment is that way," Largo said, almost calmly, pointing his massive sword through the thickest portion of the crowd.

Pirogoeth said nothing. She cursed herself for drinking any of the acrid ale, and wished she knew how Largo was able to toss aside the effects of it at need. She dipped her blade to the right, and pulled a shorter, sharper, and more ornate knife from her belt. She knew, somehow, that any magic she might attempt would have little effect on the advancing crowd. The threads and forces that she would need to pull together were not there. She could feel that she had no access to them. The presence denied her the ability to protect herself in any way other than by the knife, much like it had that day so long ago....

The crowd surged toward them with a sigh. There was no cry, no shout, just the overwhelming shuffle of bodies as they reached out and fell forward to envelop them. Largo bellowed something in a language she could not understand and hurled himself at the advancing hoard.

Pirogoeth looked up, an almost sad expression on her face. Her arm tensed as she pulled her blade back, and she could almost feel the outstretched hands as they reached mindlessly towards her.

. . .

"Aye, 'tis a shame to have had to cut down all the inhabitants of the town," Largo said as he breached a cask of ale and lifted it to his lips to drain its contents.

Pirogoeth looked forlornly at him, and then turned to look at the carnage about her. No matter how many times she saw it, the sight of so much death made her feel sick. Bodies were everywhere, but they were odd corpses, bloodless and filled with dust. She looked for items and supplies that could be of some use in their travels, but there was nothing. It was like the entire town had nothing of use, and the very life of it was only an illusion.

"Do not the bodies seem... strange?" she said, nudging the remains of what had once been the innkeeper. His bloodless corpse crumbled slightly into ashen dust as the edge of her boot touched it.

"Aye, very, but I have seen this before," Largo said, strapping what few supplies they had more firmly to the two horses they had arrived with. "Do not waste your time looking for supplies. You will find none."

She looked around. She was beginning to wonder if anything that evening had actually happened. After they had brutally cut and chopped their way out of the inn, they found the building surrounded by the rest of the townsfolk, who seemed to be suddenly, mindlessly focused on them. Their advance would not stop until they had cut down every last one of them.

Pirogoeth's back hurt, she was tired, and...she was scared. There was something horrifying about the unnatural mindlessness with which the townsfolk had come upon them. There was guilt in her hands, and what was left of her being was shaken to the core.

"Do not trouble your wee little brain about the dead," Largo said, mounting his horse. It was a huge, gray, battle-worn beast that had long ago come to terms with having Largo for its master and seemed resigned to the fact. "Not one of these folk were alive when we arrived."

A dim, foggy mist had started to roll in, leaving an unearthly gray quality to the remains of the town. It reminded her eerily of what had happened to her own city. The town was slowly fading, disappearing. Soon even the land itself would cease to exist.

"What do you mean?" she said, looking at him.

"The dead. The walking dead, that desire nothing but to feed on the living. We have a word for this in Reaht," he said, leaning ominously towards her. "We call them 'zombies.'"

"Zombies," she said, looking at him with a very flat expression. Largo had a tendency to go on in depth about things he knew nothing about, and would often invent bizarre words to explain things he didn't understand. "Zombies" sounded very much like a word he would make up.

"Yes, 'zombies,'" he said quietly, as he walked his horse over near her. The great gray's hooves sent up ashen clouds as the corpses beneath its hooves crumbled into dust. He looked down at her like she was a little child. "The walking dead. Years ago, we had conquered a small island nation off the eastern coast and were having trouble with a small fishing village on a remote corner of the island. An entire company of men went missing, and there was no trace of them to be found.

"The local inhabitants behaved very odd, and would not account for the missing men. Yet more men disappeared, and the commanders started to grow impatient with the problem. A seasoned company was dispatched to destroy the village, but only one man returned from the foray. He described a sudden change that had come over the townsfolk, a mindless, empty advance as they set upon the soldiers and started to tear at them and eat them alive. An even greater force was dispatched to deal with this, but a storm blew in from the sea and washed all traces of the village away."

He looked off into the mist. "Zombies feed on living flesh. They exist to devour the living. Yet they are only part of a greater evil. I oft wonder if that fishing village was but an experiment by this greater evil, perfecting its art on small, nameless villages before setting its plague upon the world."

There was something odd about how he told the story, which made her wonder if there might actually be some truth to it. He continued to look off into the mist, his expression somber. Then, he turned and looked down at her with a smirk.

"I somehow don't think ye would make much of a dinner for 'em, being little more than bones yourself," he said, "but these zombies woulda' eaten ye just the same. Come, let us depart. The gloomy forest awaits, and even I do not relish this road."

He spurred his horse towards the town's gloomy gates. Beyond them lay the beginnings of the dark cavernous forest and the highway that cut through it. Pirogoeth walked towards her ov horse, a small, spotted, smoke colored bea with a quiet disposition. She mounte adjusted herself in the saddle, and watch Largo's slowly departing back as he pass thru the gates.

She clucked her horse onward, reaching t gate, which seemed to be sagging a crumbling away. Then, not knowing wh she stopped and turned to look back the town.

A dark figure stood in the mist, there, b not there. For some reason, she did not fe alarmed. The figure seemed remote, as if was leagues away and this was only a di projection of it. He stood, a huge bla mantle and black robes with no hint of for under them. Long white hair fell loose acro his shoulders. She could not see his eye but she could sense them watching he One of the buildings near him in the mi creaked wearily, cracked, and crumble into dust.

She looked at him quietly. The threat th followed them was always there, even wh she could not sense it. Perhaps Largo alwa sensed it around him. For some odd reaso this comforted her. She did not need to fe it finding them, because it always knew whe they were. It stood back, waiting their ne move, as if it was all part of some amusin elaborate game.

"Pirogoeth! Come, lest I leave ye behind," Larg bellowed. She looked at his retreating back he slowly moved along the road, casual gripping the reins to his horse. She looked ba to where the figure had stood, but it was gon vanished into the mist along with the remai of the village.

Pirogoeth clucked and turned her horse ba towards the road. The tiny, almost imperceptib sound of a small bell which hung from th horse's bridle pinged quietly as she followe Largo into the gloomy forest.

~The End (for the present..

legatokyo - Volume 2 Index

his book contains strips from Chapter 1, Chapter 2, and includes extra material produced between June 01 and September 2002. For more information and more comics, visit www.megatokyo.com

ge No.	Strip Title	Date	Online Strip ID
	Chapter 01		
	Save Game?	2001-06-18	134
	Soft for a Sony	2001-06-20	135
	p0w3r pl4y	2001-06-25	137
	rejection simulation	2001-06-27	138
	the shivers	2001-07-02	140
	the hunting...	2001-07-04	141
	dead student walking	2001-07-20	149
	sad girl in mirror	2001-07-23	150
	I will teach them well	2001-07-25	151
	G.T.L. - Great Teacher Largo	2001-07-30	153
	3x1t stage right out the window	2001-08-03	154
	can't do that...	2001-08-06	155
	little miss perfection	2001-08-16	160
	making some new friends	2001-08-17	161
	have you seen this man?	2001-08-20	162
	Boo, M.D.	2001-08-24	163
	renewed faith in the platform	2001-08-28	164
	the 'direct approach'	2001-08-30	165
	an empty shell	2001-09-04	166
	personal experience	2001-09-06	167
	blood & hot air	2001-09-13	169
	too scrawny	2001-09-20	171
	Mosh Mosh Revolution	2001-09-23	172
	Power Problems	2001-09-26	173
	sudden stop	2001-09-28	174
	largo written all over it	2001-10-01	175
	the lap pour	2001-10-05	177
	j0 spid3y	2001-10-10	179
	familiar tactics	2001-10-12	180
	two orders to go	2001-10-15	181
	Privacy Threat	2001-10-17	182
	Just a little awkward	2001-10-19	183
	nothing to worry about	2001-10-22	184
	we have met the enemy	2001-10-24	185
	heh, it's not a game	2001-10-29	187
	that kind of gaijin	2001-11-02	189
	Stray Rounds	2001-11-05	190
	conscience conundrum	2001-11-10	192
	omake: Leave it to Seraphim!	2001-11-14	194
	Chapter 02		
	Chapter 2: things change little by little.	2001-11-19	196
	Breakfast, Lunch & Turtles	2001-11-21	197
	privacy algorithms	2001-11-25	198
	Sheet Metal	2001-11-28	199
	Less than honest	2001-12-03	201
	hard to get out of	2001-12-05	202
	c2-dead piro day #1 - 'left behind'	2001-12-07	203
	back to that day	2001-12-10	204
	Handcuffed by Mounties!	2001-12-17	206
	Trust Me	2001-12-19	207
	Dumpster Diving	2002-01-04	211
	manga-ka ja nai	2002-01-07	212
	Canadian English is Better English	2002-01-09	213
	my dumpster is my temple	2002-01-23	215
	her version	2002-01-25	216
	last night i what?	2002-01-28	217
	hunting without weapons	2002-01-30	218
	nothing but grays	2002-02-01	219
	quit while you're ahead	2002-02-06	221
	Ninja Doll System	2002-02-11	223
	i dont feel like playing	2002-02-18	226
	DPD: MegaWinter Nights - Endgames	2002-02-25	229
	appearances are everything	2002-02-27	230
	finishing moves	2002-03-04	231
	small changes	2002-03-06	232
	better than shopping	2002-03-08	233
	Signing Bonuses	2002-03-11	234
	where is the 3vil one?	2002-03-13	235
	Falling Darkly	2002-03-15	236
	what mockery is this?	2002-03-18	237
	an ending without honor	2002-03-20	238
	DPD: Endgames 2	2002-03-22	239
	rejection assumptions	2002-03-25	240
	endgames turning	2002-03-27	241
	evil runes	2002-04-01	243
	beach landing	2002-04-03	244
	Virtual Friends	2002-04-05	245
	a flair for incidents	2002-04-10	247
	pure disgust	2002-04-12	248
	so pathetic	2002-04-15	249

Page No.	Strip Title	Date	Online Strip ID
88	the question	2002-04-17	250
89	little fan club	2002-04-24	251
90	little plastic peices	2002-04-29	252
91	DPD: All this sorrow becomes me	2002-05-01	253
92	art supplies	2002-05-03	254
93	EdQuake	2002-05-06	255
94	make bad man go away	2002-05-08	256
95	bad impressions	2002-05-13	258
96	the taste of failure	2002-05-15	259
97	pinging angels	2002-05-17	260
98	empty vessels	2002-05-20	261
99	seiyuu lessons	2002-05-24	263
100	could have been worse	2002-05-27	264
101	B4thing in b33r	2002-06-14	272
102	respawning tactics	2002-06-17	273
103	my l33t senses never tingle wrong	2002-06-21	275
104	my treat this time	2002-06-24	276
105	yakusoku	2002-06-26	277
106	they came to destroy...	2002-06-28	278
107	it's raining zombies!!	2002-07-03	280
108	n3kt4r of the godz	2002-07-08	282
109	undeading conversation	2002-07-10	283
110	cheap fantasies	2002-07-15	285
111	Camping the Medipak	2002-07-17	286
112	The end was n3ar	2002-07-22	288
113	my cool thing!	2002-07-24	289
114	Stoppu!!	2002-08-05	293
115	Rampage Permit	2002-08-07	294
116	post mortem confession	2002-08-09	295
117	r4ck3d	2002-08-12	296
118	the 3v1l device beckons	2002-08-16	298
119	as you wish, prissywings	2002-08-19	299
120	angelic body attack!	2002-08-21	300
121	and that was enough for now...	2002-08-23	301
122	Cordless Headshot	2002-09-02	305
123	Seraphim Check! - of powder and pixles	2002-09-04	306

Shirt Guy Dom strips

Page No.	Strip Title	Date	Online Strip ID
125	dom does baltimore	2001-09-18	170
127	SGD: ed and dom's big adventure	2001-11-07	191
128	SGD: Trepanning for Dummies	2002-02-20	227
129	Telling it like it isn't	2002-03-29	242
130	more weird for your dollar	2002-05-10	257
131	SGD - Cosplayer Zombie Hoard Bloodbath	2002-07-01	279
132	SGD: MegaTokyo walkthrough!	2002-08-26	302

One-Shot (non-story) Episodes

Page No.	Strip Title	Date	Online Strip ID
133	Doko Kana Megatokyo!	2002-02-15	225
134	Naze Nani MT: Of Trolls & Flames	2002-02-04	220
135	Mammoth Cave Incident	2001-07-18	148
137	wtc disaster: a failure of conscience	2001-09-11	168
138	Happy Holidays	2001-12-25	208
139	Leave it to Seraphim! - comic analysis	2002-05-31	266
140	halloween special - daydream before	2001-10-31	188
141	Bioware Day - Today on 'Largo'	2001-11-30	200
142	attack of the hosting hobgoblins	2002-01-21	214
143	packing away	2002-02-13	224
144	OSE: Sticky Boxes	2002-07-12	284
145	OSE: MT year 2: Gomen nasai	2002-08-14	297
146	omake: lazy piro and his laptop	2001-11-12	193
147	can't find dom day - 'the death star'	2001-12-12	205

Dead Piro Art Days

Page No.	Strip Title	Date	Online Strip ID
149	DPD: Discarded Frames	2002-08-02	292
150	Guest Strip Contest	2001-06-29	139
151	dead piro day - seraphim & boo	2001-10-03	176
152	Piro Art Day - 002	2001-07-28	152
153	'warmth' - non-MT art day	2001-10-08	178
154	omake: just a kimiko sketch	2001-11-16	195
155	DPD: Piro's Sketchbook #1	2002-04-08	246
156	DPD: Waiting for the Show	2002-07-26	290
157	DPD: feild cleaning (1 of 4)	2002-06-05	268
158	DPD: Yuzo Takada Tribute	2002-06-07	269
159	DPD: Dance of the Evils	2002-06-10	270
160	DPD: but my wings are only small wings	2002-06-12	271
161	DPD: no data can fill the empty spaces	2002-06-19	274
162	evil has many guises	2002-07-19	287
163	DPD: kotone from 'sight'	2002-02-08	222
164	DPD: a girl of nothing but greys	2002-05-22	262
165	DPD: Brownfields, Greyfields	2002-08-28	303

Megatokyo Gamewords

Page No.	Strip Title	Date	Online Strip ID
167	Capture the Bear	2002-01-02	210
168	Inn of the Prancing Pirogoeth	2002-08-30	304
169	DPD: Endgames Standing	2002-07-05	281
170	Pirogoeth	2001-08-13	158

This is the back of the book!

For cryin' out loud, people — *Megatokyo* was originally done in ENGLISH, so it NATURALLY reads LEFT to RIGHT! You know, the way you learned in school? Now, turn the book over and start at the front. Jeez.

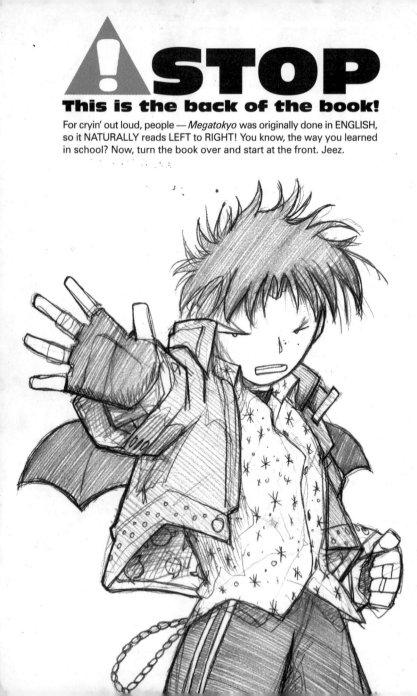